What Unites
Presbyterians

What Unites Presbyterians

Common Ground for Troubled Times

Clifton Kirkpatrick

William H. Hopper, Jr.

Geneva Press
Louisville, Kentucky

Book and cover design
by Jennifer K. Cox

First edition
Published by Geneva Press
Louisville, Kentucky

This book is printed on acid-free paper that meets the
American National Standards Institute Z39.48 standard. ∞

PRINTED IN THE UNITED STATES OF AMERICA
97 98 99 00 01 02 03 04 05 06 — 10 9 8 7 6 5 4 3 2 1

Library of Congress Cataloging-in-Publication Data

Kirkpatrick, Clifton, 1945–
    What unites Presbyterians : common ground for troubled times /
  Clifton Kirkpatrick, William H. Hopper, Jr.
         p.   cm.
    Includes bibliographical references and index.
    ISBN 0-664-50007-2 (alk. paper)
    1. Presbyterian Church (U.S.A.) I. Hopper, William H., 1925–
  II. Title.
  BX8969.2.K57 1997
  285'.137—dc21   97-19427

To Diane W. Kirkpatrick,
builder of houses, families, and communities and the love of my life,
and to three very special young adults who mean the world to us:
our son, David,
our daughter—and PC(USA) pastor—Elizabeth,
our son-in-law, Rowly

To Mollie B. Hopper,
loving, caring, and supportive wife for nearly half a century,
and to our wonderful three young 'uns, Laura, Jane, Mary Ann,
who aren't so young anymore,
and to their terrific life partners,
and to the three marvelous grandsons, John, Reed, Jason

Contents

Preface

Before they were elected to their respective positions at the 208th General Assembly (1996) of the Presbyterian Church (U.S.A.) in Albuquerque, New Mexico, John Buchanan, who became moderator, and Clifton Kirkpatrick, who became stated clerk, discussed the need for finding common ground in an increasingly divided church. They saw the Common Ground Project, begun by Cardinal Bernardin of the Roman Catholic Church, as a possible model.

Also deeply concerned over divisions and the need for healing in the church, president John Mulder of Louisville Presbyterian Theological Seminary urged Cliff Kirkpatrick, long identified with the mission of the church, to write a book about what unites Presbyterians.

Agreeing that such a book needed to be written, Cliff realized that his official responsibilities and extensive meeting, writing, and speaking schedules would make such a demanding undertaking impossible without help. Accordingly, at the end of October 1996, Cliff telephoned a retired former colleague in mission and former neighbor in Louisville, Bill Hopper, to coauthor such a book with him.

When a formal proposal was taken to Davis Perkins, the President and Publisher of the Presbyterian Publishing Corporation, Davis concurred that such a book was urgently needed and that every effort should be made to have the book published before the 209th General Assembly, to convene on June 14, 1997.

One further note of interest. Early in the process it seemed to the coauthors and editor that no other book quite like this one on the Presbyterian Church (U.S.A.) had ever been written, combining the Reformed tradition, theology, worship, and mission at all governing body levels. It was then decided to try to make this book accessible and helpful for a quick overview of American Presbyterianism and its roots for new (and continuing) church members, church officers, and seminary students. Thus, this is not a technical book but a practical one for all who care deeply about the American Presbyterian branch of the church of Jesus Christ.

Acknowledgments

No author or authors ever wrote a book in isolation. In this case, wherein the coauthors live hundreds of miles apart, close touch and communication was maintained through Joyce Evans, administrative assistant in the Office of the General Assembly. Joyce cared so much that she made helpful suggestions along the way; we are grateful to her!

Suggested reading, ideas for consideration, and great encouragement were provided by many, but we wish to mention these few particularly: Lois and George Cole, Gwen Crawley, Barry Creech, Miriam Dunson, Jack Hutchison, Curtis A. Kearns, Jr., Lewis Lancaster, Hedy and Bob Lodwick, Brad Longfield, Gary Luhr, Barbara and Bob Miller, James F. Moore, John Mulder, Davis Perkins, Eunice Poethig, Sonnie Swentson, and Wanda and Arch Taylor.

Grateful acknowledgment is made to the following for permission to reproduce copyrighted material.

Jane Parker Huber, for "Called as Partners in Christ's Service," © 1981 by Jane Parker Huber, from her book *A Singing Faith* (Philadelphia: Westminster Press, 1987).

Westminster John Knox Press, for "God of Our Life," by Hugh Thomson Kerr, © 1928, renewed © 1956 by the Presbyterian Board of Christian Education.

1

What Unites Presbyterians
The Need for Common Ground

Our subject is the experience of the Presbyterian Church (U.S.A.), with its heritage from other countries and its relationships with partner churches in the United States and around the world. At this time in the history of our church it is particularly important for us to recognize our common ground, the ties that bind, as we face a whole host of complicated issues, many of which are new, at least in their present form.

We believe that many of our company will be surprised and delighted to recognize anew the broad swath of common ground on which we stand—and from which we seek to go forward in mission and in ministry. Each succeeding chapter will feature one portion of our common mosaic. It is an exciting and challenging time, even in the midst of differences, to anticipate a new Pentecost.

The Bible

Presbyterians properly seek to garner truth, wisdom, and guidance in the pages of the Bible. Being dogmatic about the precise meaning of the Bible in any particular passage can be dangerous, but the tenor of the message in the seventeenth chapter of the Gospel of John seems clear. Eugene Peterson, in *The Message*, gives this rendering of John 17:20–21:

> The goal is for all of them to become one heart and mind—
> Just as you, Father, are in me and I in you,
> So they might be one heart and mind with us.
> Then the world might believe that you, in fact, sent me.[1]

In short, the unity of the brothers and sisters of the faith with each other, and with God in Jesus Christ, is clearly related to the proclamation and the acceptance of the gospel. Unity is not an abstract thought with some unattached virtue. In the more familiar language of Jesus' prayer in the NRSV, the text is: "that they may all be one . . . so that the world may believe" (John 17:21). That is potent language! Unity enables a common vision of mission.

What is sometimes called Jesus' high-priestly prayer in the Garden (in John 17) directly relates the gospel proclaimed with the gospel lived, that is, with "one heart and mind." We need to get on with our work, and that work can best be accomplished when we are working in tandem.

Another series of passages from the book of Acts helps us to focus on the power of God as evidenced in the church. Those early believers seemed like revolutionaries who turned the world upside down (see Acts 17:6). And who were these people? They were "Parthians, Medes, Elamites, and residents of Mesopotamia, Judea and Cappadocia, Pontus and Asia, Phrygia and Pamphylia, Egypt and the parts of Libya belonging to Cyrene, and visitors from Rome, both Jews and proselytes, Cretans and Arabs . . ." (Acts 2:9–11). That is to say, they were from Africa, Europe, and Asia; of different nations, races, and languages; and from various interest groups, to use our current idiom. They cooperated and the gospel was eloquently proclaimed. They heard, they believed, and they witnessed!

All biblical students are aware of the growth from an exclusive band of Jewish followers to a diverse and inclusive church of an increasing variety of persons from many nations and cultures. Today the Presbyterian Church (U.S.A.)—and that means every member of every congregation—unites in relating to partner churches in over eighty countries around the world.

The theme of unity in the faith is further illustrated in 1 Corinthians 12:7–12, where we read how each member is given an aspect of the Spirit for the common good; gifts of wisdom, knowledge, faith, healing, miracle-working, prophecy, the discernment of spirits, speaking in tongues, and interpretation of tongues are distributed, for "just as the body is one and has many members, and all the members of the body, though many, are one body, so it is with Christ" (v. 12). The foot, the hand, the ear, the eye, and all the other parts make one body. We have different backgrounds, different perspectives, and different worldviews, but we come together in Jesus Christ to be used by God—as one whole!

Early Compromises for Unity in the Church in the United States

The history of the Presbyterian Church in this country is not without instruction for us to consider. In a very real sense, the birth of the Presbyterian Church in this country was the result of a split from an established church in Europe in the period of the American Revolution. Most Presbyterians today would insist that it was essential for those who came to this country to establish the religious freedom needed to reject the restrictive forms of the official practices of Christianity in a European nation—just as Luther and Calvin had felt the need to seek to reform the Roman Catholic Church in the sixteenth century because of its perceived corrupt nature and false teachings. There *are* times when some kinds of division are necessary when a fundamental principle is at stake that is not just pertinent, but so vital to the witness of the gospel that, with Luther, one must say, "Here I stand. I can do no other."[2]

Few Presbyterians today are aware of some of the compromises that had to be made for the unity of Presbyterians of somewhat different thinking and convictions before the formation of the first General Assembly in Philadelphia in 1789 (at the same time that the first National Congress was meeting in New York). What has been called the Adopting Act of 1729 provided that ministers in the Presbyterian Church had to accept the Westminster Confession of Faith and the Larger and Shorter Catechisms (all in our current *Book of Confessions*[3]) "as being in all the essential and necessary articles, good forms of sound words and systems of Christian doctrine."[4] What saved this original unity for Presbyterians in the United States was not uniformity, since each minister who could not accept every word of what was written in London in 1649 could list "scruples" about any particular part of what had been adopted at Westminster. The compromise was that subscription to a precise theological structure was not mandatory.

Even with the spirit of compromise and tolerance, however, there was a split in 1741 between the "Old Side" and the "New Side," and there is little doubt that one casualty was a unified witness in mission on the western frontier—the "West" being such places as the Blue Ridge Mountains and Pittsburgh, Pennsylvania. Happily, that schism was healed in 1758.

At the formation of the General Assembly in 1789, it was determined that each minister must answer this question: "Do you sincerely receive and adopt the Confession of Faith of this church (the Westminster Confession), as containing the system of doctrine taught in the Holy Scriptures?"[5] It is significant that in the beginning there was no exact formulation of doctrine; unity was deemed more important than theological conformity. Purity in the church has seldom been "the" most important principle.

Then came the "Old School" and the "New School" split in 1837, but the next major schism after that one was not healed in a mere seventeen years. At the time of the Civil War in 1861, the Presbyterian Church in the Confederate States of America (later the Presbyterian Church in the United States, commonly called the Southern Church) left the Presbyterian Church in the U.S.A., and that rupture was not finally healed until 122 years later, in 1983. Along the way, there were other unions among the various Presbyterian denominations. Two are of particular interest to us today.

The Cumberland Presbyterian Church was formed on the frontier of Tennessee and Kentucky because of the requirement of a seminary education for all pastors, as practiced in the Presbyterian Church in the U.S.A.—and because of objection to predestination as stated in the Westminster Confession.

The Cumberland Church decided that there were too few seminary graduates to pastor all of the developing clusters of people "in the West." Division was thought necessary by those who formed the Cumberland Presbyterian Church so that people on the frontier could have religious leadership from pastors and preachers, even though the formal educational qualifications for those ministers were less than might be desired. The reunion between some Cumberland churches and the Presbyterian Church in the U.S.A. occurred in 1906.[6]

Further, "dissenters" from Scotland and northern Ireland, who were often called Covenanters or Seceders, settled in New York, South Carolina, and southeastern Pennsylvania before moving to western Pennsylvania. They preserved many of their convictions and worship practices, singing only psalms, for instance. The two largest of these groups, which were the Associate Reformed Presbyterian Church (excepting one synod) and the Associate Presbyterian Church, merged in 1858 to form the United Presbyterian Church of North America. The United Presbyterian Church and the Presbyterian Church in the U.S.A. came together in 1958 in Pittsburgh. Harmony in a larger fellowship took place in each instance.

With its report in 1927 to the General Assembly of the Presbyterian Church in the U.S.A., the Commission of 1925 recommended, and the General Assembly "adopted unanimously without debate," the deletion of the established criteria that a minister previously had to accept to be ordained.[7] The conservatives who were the majority at that time took that action to keep the liberals in the church! The conservatives' heretofore-prized "fundamentals" would be eliminated from any required subscription statement for the sake of unity.

What can be learned from the previous divisions and unions in the Presbyterian family? Not all would agree on the lessons from earlier divisions, but we suggest several of importance: (a) Division can be harmful for the witness to Jesus Christ. Bitter debates and recriminations are not likely to bring serenity and peace. Jesus prayed that his followers would be one. (b) Any church member who is sensitive can observe that time, money, and energy devoted to fighting and dividing is taking time, energy, and money away from other causes that are the true reasons for the existence of the church. (c) The third result of ecclesiastical infighting is also obvious. In trying to win points and consolidate positions, people begin to question the motives—and the commitment to Jesus Christ—of those with whom they disagree; invective often replaces reasoned dialogue, and tensions become so aroused that Christian charity and objectivity become lost. In terminology from psychology and the social sciences, the situation becomes a lose-lose instead of a win-win result, so that everyone loses even if one side is declared the winner by receiving more votes in a church governing body in the particular debate or argument.

"Winning" in Christ's Name

In addition to the appeal to scripture and concrete experience, peace and unity are important so that the church's focus does not become distorted. The problem always looms that instead of emphasizing the mission of the church, two or more contending sides might become absorbed in identifying themselves with a winning cause. Obediently following Jesus' command to witness in all the world is difficult enough without adding the burden of internal squabbling, which leads nowhere but to the torpedoing of the purity of the message of the love of God. Any determination of churchwide evangelism or mission advance can be held hostage to the forces that demand a battle to the death over the correctness of one's position.

The late Cardinal Bernardin of Chicago was the moving spirit behind a Roman Catholic effort to find "common ground" to try to reduce polarization in "a renewed spirit of civility, dialogue, generosity, and broad and serious consultation."[8] There is nothing whatever wrong with diversity; in fact, diversity within the fellowship can be a sign of grace, freedom, and love. A recent Roman Catholic paper[9] points out that "When we . . . recognize that no single group or viewpoint in the church has a complete monopoly on the truth":

We should not envision ourselves or any one part of
the church a saving remnant. . . .
We should presume that those with whom we differ
are acting in good faith. They deserve civility, charity,
and a good faith effort to understand their concerns. We
should not substitute labels . . . for complicated realities.
We should put the best possible construction on differing positions. . . .
We should be cautious in ascribing motives. We
should not impugn another's love of the church and loy-
alty to it.[10]

The Results of Division

One result is always potentially present: a split leads to another split, to another split, as those who came together to
abolish a common enemy now learn that there is division
within the new party of "purity." A group decides to work
with other like-minded people who are convinced that the denomination is wrong in its theology, polity, or biblical interpretation, or terribly unwise in a specific decision or action,
but when the united group splits off, different shades of perspectives and thinking emerge. So to be absolutely correct,
some in the new group split again—it was so easy to do the
first time. Finally, only the two of us are left, and, quite frankly,
there is some question about you!

Outsiders can have nothing but pain and sadness as they
witness the great trauma that Southern Baptists are enduring
as they participate in titanic struggles for control of the Southern Baptist Convention and its seminaries.

In Christ all kinds of things are possible when there is mutual respect and trust. Let us look to Paul in Romans 15:1–7 for
an understanding of mutual support in unity: "Those of us
who are strong and able in the faith need to step in and lend a
hand to those who falter, and not just do what is most conve-
nient for us. Strength is for service, not status. Each one of us

needs to look after the good of the people around us, asking ourselves, 'How can I help?'"[11] Paul goes on to urge the Christians to live in harmony, so that together they may glorify God. Unity is not for the sake of the community, but for the glory of God! The implication is clear: Dis-unity is not for the glory of God, and it is the worst kind of witness.

"In a famous letter to Archbishop Cranmer, John Calvin declared that the disunity of the church was to be ranked as one of the great evils of the time. '. . . the members of the Church being severed, the body is bleeding. So much does this concern me that, could I be of any service, I would not grudge to cross even ten seas, if need were on account of it.'"[12] The call to find common ground is for the cause of Jesus Christ! We are united in knowing Christ as Lord. We are united in acknowledging the authority of scripture. We are united in our *Book of Confessions*. We are united in a deep appreciation for Presbyterian polity. We are united in mission, past and present. We have, indeed, a common ground from which to discuss difficult and controversial issues with one another in Christian love!

Presbyterians have never been known for hiding their heads in the sand, so there is no point in our saying that we agree on everything. We definitely do not, and we all know it! At the very heart of our doing things "decently and in order," however, is the way in which we *disagree*, as well as the ways we agree. We need not be shy about how and why and where we take a stand, but there are at least two cautions we observe when we have internal struggles. First—and the announced theme of this book—is to be fully aware and appreciative of what unites us. In our vigorous and forthright discussions, and even confrontations, we dare not ignore the broad and deep range of the realities that bind us very close together.

The second undergirding principle for us in our times of internal discord is to be sensitive to and care for each other. That means that we must not question or demean the fundamental integrity of the other person or persons. As we debate with conviction, based upon our reading of scripture, our theology, experience, pastoral care, and our understanding of a God of love, so we must assert to ourselves and to others that we believe that they operate from the same motives, principles, and beliefs as ours. That also means that we do not become personal. It is very easy to say that we hate another's ideas, but love the person; but acting upon these words is difficult. Further, we must agree not to distort any position that is not our own, being scrupulously fair in stating another's words or position. All of that also means that we *listen* to the best of our ability to what others are saying and feeling, not being so wrapped up in our own rebuttal that we turn off insights and glimpses of truth that might otherwise be ours.

In the following chapters we shall seek to call attention to a rich variety of ways in which our unity is displayed: the centrality of our foundation in Jesus Christ; our determination as a sinful people to be in an ongoing process to reform the church; our belief in the sovereignty of God; our conviction that every human being has to do with the living God every moment. We review our basic commitment to the "preliminary principles" in the *Book of Order*: Jesus Christ as living Lord, the Head of the Church; the centrality of the Bible; the *Book of Confessions*. We then turn to the Great Ends of the Church: the proclamation of the gospel; the spiritual fellowship of the church; divine worship; the preservation of truth; and the promotion of social righteousness. The Historic Principles of Church Order are followed by the Historic Principles of Church Government, and our acceptance of the Constitution of the Church, including the three parts of the *Book of Order*: (1) the Form of Government, (2) the Directory for Worship and (3) the Rules of Discipline; and the *Book of Confessions*. The confessions and what it means to be a confessional church also bind us together in a remarkable manner.

Our understanding of mission is one of the great bonding aspects of the Presbyterian Church (U.S.A.): mission past, and mission present; mission to every corner of the United States, and mission to a whole host of countries around the planet; mission to and with people; mission in a variety of ways that form a beautiful tapestry of care and concern for people of all races and nationalities. In short, mission is a vital reason for being. Presbyterians are only one part of the totality of God's people, so an exploration of unity increases our understanding of who we are and shapes our understanding of mission. Even diversity in mission is perfectly all right and acceptable. A closer look at the centrality of scripture and the implications for us all comes next. Again and again we return to the core that unites us in Jesus Christ and in the scriptures, how we interpret scripture, how scripture guides us, and how we apply scripture both individually and corporately. A binding subject that appears repeatedly is our Reformed worship, including the basic elements of prayer, preaching, the sacraments, liturgy and music, and the offering of ourselves and of our substance. A section on national and global mission shows what we have done together as a church, the directions we have taken, and where we might be headed.

St. John's-by-the-Gas-Station is our language for the particular church, our constitutional term for local congregation. We have a truly amazing agreement about what congregations should be and what congregational mission should be; we believe that that aspect of our life together should also be celebrated.

Nearly everyone applauds our polity (our system of governance), so in our rejoicing we highlight the virtues and values of the representative, democratic, open way in which we conduct ourselves, noting that the way we engage in process is often as significant as whatever the resulting plans adopted, persons elected or ordained, or major decisions may be. Toward the end we list a surprising litany of small ways in which we unassumingly illustrate our unity. We conclude with visions that are not unique to us. Our hope is that in our being together in the implementation of common visions our love for one another will be manifest. The more we are intentional about our desire for cooperative living, the more we can justly attest to the kind of loving and caring God we proclaim. With zeal and enthusiasm we can do far more than we know or think possible to be the people who we believe God intends us to be as we join in working at the tasks that God calls us to do.

Common ground gives us the strength in a loving spirit to discuss difficult issues, about which we may have quite divergent opinions with one another, and yet to undertake difficult tasks in a corporate manner.

We now turn to the magnificent convictions and practices that have bound us together in Christian faith and mission, and about which we sing:

The church's one foundation
Is Jesus Christ her Lord;
She is His new creation
By water and the word;
From heaven He came and sought her
To be His holy bride;
With His own blood He bought her,
And for her life He died.

Elect from every nation,
Yet one o'er all the earth,
Her charter of salvation
One Lord, one faith, one birth;
One holy name she blesses,
Partakes one holy food,
And to one hope she presses,
With every grace endued.

. . . .

Yet she on earth has union
With God the Three in One,
And mystic sweet communion
With those whose rest is won:
O happy ones and holy!
Lord, give us grace that we,
Like them, the meek and lowly,
May live eternally.

(Samuel John Stone)[13]

2

It Is Important to Choose One's Ancestors with Care
Our Reformed Heritage

Perhaps the Reformed tradition should be discarded! It is not new; it is not improved; it does not come in a larger size; it does not come in a new package; and perhaps worst of all, its price has not been reduced—nothing is on sale at bargain rates. Obviously, there is no market for it—right?

Before discarding the Reformed heritage completely, however, let us first examine what we mean by our Reformed heritage in tradition and in theology. Among other things, our ancestors have claimed these four key thoughts.

Our bedrock faith is in God in Jesus Christ

There is no dispute about our foundation. All Presbyterians give a ringing endorsement to the centrality of Jesus Christ, who is at the center of our faith; we start there.

This is to say, the heritage of the members of the Presbyterian Church (U.S.A.) begins with God in Jesus Christ; and that heritage includes all Christians in one holy, catholic, apostolic church. We particularly relate, of course, to the entire Protestant community, especially through our own denomination, and closer to home, to our own particular church. This is our heritage, and we must confess that "every tradition has its share of false starts, mistaken judgments, and betrayal of its own convictions,"[1] but whether one, or one hundred, or one thousand, or one hundred thousand, we would surely wish to reflect a long time before trying to change our ancestral lineage. We chose our ancestors well!

We do well to establish early on, then, that our Reformed heritage did not begin in the sixteenth century, but it has its roots firmly planted in the soil of Iraq, Israel, Egypt, and the entire Mediterranean Basin of the biblical period, and our branches are currently spread over every continent. Some of our particularities stem from central Europe in the sixteenth century, but even in that swath of European geography we must be careful to include the Bohemia of John Huss (part of today's Czech Republic) and the Germany of Martin Luther as well as the Switzerland of Huldrych Zwingli and John Calvin, the England of the Westminster Assembly, and certainly the Scotland of John Knox.

We must never forget the three fundamental tenets that emerged from the germinal thinking of Martin Luther in the Reformation, beginning in 1517. Others in addition to these three arc also highly significant, so we need to look at a broad range of basic convictions that arose from the Protestant Reformation.

First, Martin Luther's biblical studies led him to reject outright the teaching of the Roman Catholic Church that the church, whether through pope or priest, could somehow provide salvation. The foil was a man named Tetzel who was selling indulgences, or forgiveness from sin, so that a person already dead could be released from the clutches of Satan and be permitted to pass from purgatory into heaven. Luther considered this practice to be a contradiction of the New Testament, particularly the teachings of the apostle Paul, found clearly, Luther taught, in the letters to the Romans and to the Galatians. The New Testament theme came to be called "justification by faith," in contrast to justification through a seemingly magical act of the church.[2]

The second principle was almost a corollary of the first: Only scripture is authoritative, not the church or the teachings of the church. In fact, each Christian could interpret the Bible so that it was not necessary, and certainly not essential, for scripture to be interpreted by the church through pope, church council, or priest. John Calvin stressed—as the Reformed church has ever since—the absolute necessity for Bible study. It is just a few more steps until we arrive at the Reformed emphasis upon an educated ministry, and further, a keen and steady urgency about Christian education in general for all people. The preaching of the word, understandably in these terms, has characterized Reformed worship, and the term formerly in use, which referred to ministers as "teaching elders," signified the importance of this aspect of church life. A United Negro College Fund television commercial that has run in the 1990s states, "The mind is a terrible thing to waste." With slight adjustments, this commercial could be used to apply to the Presbyterian Church, which has endorsed and provided quality education through its own church schools, the numerous Presbyterian church colleges, campus ministries, and theological education. Historically the denomination has repeatedly and firmly supported public education.

This insight about education for all led, among other things, to Martin Luther's third key principle: the priesthood of all believers. Every Christian should have the privilege, or rather, the duty and responsibility to study, learn, and interpret the Bible. The inevitable conclusion was that it was not necessary to seek the special interpretation of the church and its priests, since each Christian, acting on his or her own, could interpret the Bible. The priesthood of all believers also means that each Christian should be a priest for every other person through witness, prayer, and pastoral care and for ameliorating the gifts of God. Confession to a priest was not a requirement, since every Christian could pray all kinds of prayers, including confession, directly to God.

Ecclesia reformata, semper reformanda

The church reformed [is] always being reformed (under the Word of God). The early Protestant Reformers did not perceive of themselves as creating a new denomination, and certainly not a new religion. They were convinced that the medieval church was corrupt in a number of ways, so they sought to change it, to reform it. The Protestant Reformation meant two things. The Protestants *protested* against the church that they knew. The medieval church was not what the Protestants understood a New Testament church should be. But the word "protest" means not just to object to something. "Protest" comes from the two Latin words *pro*, meaning "for," and *testari* or "testify," meaning "to speak for," or "to testify for." Thus, the Protestant Reformers wanted to state, or testify to, what they believed the church of Jesus Christ should be! At its best, the Reformed church is always seeking to change (to reform) from whatever is not right to whatever is correct. The purpose was—and is—to make right those things that were, or are, wrong in the church. We agree fundamentally that change is necessary, but we do not always agree on what or how to change.

How fortunate we are to be heirs of an "open posture," rather than of a closed society, or one in which some of our kindred brothers and sisters writhe, where there is virtually no freedom to maneuver in giving vent to one's heartfelt convictions or to explore the implications of various possibilities in the pursuit of yet undiscovered or unstated truth. A mission study tour heard a professor at the historic Reformed Seminary in Debrecen, Hungary, say after the end of the communist era: "Our greatest task is to learn to live in freedom!" We begin by recognizing that God has still not completely revealed God's self; or, to put the issue in another way, we have not yet grasped fully what God is seeking to say to us or to teach us. That is why, together, we are always searching for the leading of God.

God is sovereign

A belief in the sovereignty of God has often been called the basic theological conviction for John Calvin. The ramifications of that doctrine radiate out in several directions. The noteworthy

Presbyterian belief in predestination flows as a direct result of belief in an all-powerful and almighty God who has created the universe and all of us creatures in it, and who remains in control. That sovereign God in grace and steadfast love has brought redemption to humankind. Furthermore, if God is preeminent, God's creatures are not—so the obvious limitations of human beings should not be surprising. A concomitant understanding from Genesis, then, is that human beings have sought, also, to be godlike with infinite knowledge and "control," and consequently humans have rebelled against God in desiring to be like God. Call it original sin, or just sin.

Modern Presbyterians may have more problems in naming themselves as sinful creatures than have earlier generations, but belief in a sovereign God stipulates that humans are not God. Sometimes grudgingly, but honestly, we have concurred that we are sinful creatures. The positive side of that has been helpfully explained, as we further accept God's grace and forgiveness:

[I]f sin means derangement, grace means rearrangement. If sin means the brokenness of human relationships to each other and to God, then grace means the transforming divine power and initiative that overcomes brokenness and that elicits a new responsiveness to God and neighbor. Grace means regeneration: the conversion, restoration, and rehabilitation of faithful participants in the divine commonwealth. Grace means the renewal of genuine communion. Where the probability of grace goes unrecognized, so too does the promise of persons, communities, and institutions.[3]

A person reading through the *Book of Confessions* the first time could easily be astounded by the repeated references to "the one God." We are used to saying and hearing, "I believe in God . . . almighty, maker of heaven and earth" in the Apostles' Creed. But in the Scots Confession, the opening line is, "We confess and acknowledge one God alone . . . ," and very clearly the king of England was not God. The Heidelberg Catechism taught that God had called, elected, and provided salvation. The emperor of the Holy Roman Empire was surely not God. In the Theological Declaration of Barmen, the state or Adolf Hitler was not God. Calvin forcefully taught that *nothing else* is God—God is sovereign. No church, no investment portfolio, no handsome or beautiful spouse, no possession of any kind, no child is sovereign; God is sovereign. Everything else is relative.

If, then, a sovereign God decides to elect persons to eternal life, that is a decision for all time and eternity, and salvation or redemption is pure grace because no one is made righteous by deed or thought (faith), or deserves salvation, because all have sinned and have fallen short of the glory of God. People are thus *predestined* to life eternal, that is, a quality of life with God.

Presbyterians have endorsed this conviction, but with Calvin, we have always had trouble with it for two reasons. First, if God predestines every person, and not all are called, elected, or predestined for salvation, then God has predestined (the Westminster Confession says "fore-ordained") some persons to hell or eternal damnation. Second, if God has determined the ultimate fate of all persons, then the individual has no power to make any important decisions. Presbyterians have learned to believe, also, in free will, realizing that these two doctrines are logically impossible to hold at the same time, but that each is true, as taught in the Westminster Confession.[4]

Those persons who can with a clear conscience accept what they are taught, regardless of apparent inconsistencies, are in some ways better off than those who think. It is almost unfortunate that Presbyterians are a thinking people; life might be easier if we did not worry so much about some things. Obviously, there is a tension between both asserting that God has determined everything and believing that humans have free wills to make their own decisions—even to do what is wrong. There is always a creative tension between these two because we *do* believe both, even when we know that they are logically inconsistent. The conviction that God not only predestines, but predestines some to damnation, is called double predestination, and most Presbyterians have great trouble in accepting that possibility. We refuse to accept any teaching that some persons not only have no choice, but they do not even have any chance, that they are doomed to eternal punishment.

Our situation has one virtue: Our problem is at the right place in our system of thinking and believing. We are convinced that God loves us, cares for us, wishes everyone to have a quality of life now and forever with God (eternal life in the Gospel of John), but we also believe that God has made us free creatures.

Every human being has to do with the *living* God at every moment

It is not quite accurate to say that John Calvin "added" additional key points to the Reformation principles, but it is true that Calvin emphasized other issues, as well as those promulgated by Luther. John H. Leith, for instance, maintains that the central theme of Calvinist theology, which holds it all together, is that every human being has to do with the living God at every moment. Leith writes, "The glory of God and [God's] purposes in the world are more important than the salvation of one's own soul. *Personal salvation can be a very selfish act*" (emphasis added).[5]

"Those Calvinists who asked candidates for the ministry if they were willing to be damned for the glory of God were trying to root out the last element of self-seeking in religion."[6] Stories abound about the very tough grilling and the difficult questions that a candidate had to answer before presbytery. Finally on one occasion a presbyter asked the candidate: "Would you be willing to be damned for the glory of God?" The candidate quickly responded: "Moderator, I would be willing for the whole presbytery to be damned for the glory of God!"

Let us not allow any somewhat humorous recollections to deter us from thinking clearly about the importance of living all of life to the glory of God. Such things as the teaching about

Sabbath observance in an earlier era than ours meant refraining from activities on Sunday that were for wanton pleasure, not done to magnify God. The first question and answer in the Westminster Shorter Catechism can pose an awkward dilemma as it deals with both God and delight. "What is the chief end of man [sic]?" "Man's chief end is to glorify God, and to enjoy Him forever."[7] A beautiful contemporary rephrasing of that thought is, "Our chief end . . . is to enjoy communion with God in community with others."[8] There is a rhythm to life, and many of us seem not to have discerned new ways to claim sacred hours in each week for meditation, reflection, reading, or reveling in the beauty of God's creation as we sing a new song of thanksgiving and praise.

Related to the theme of living life to the glory of God and Sabbath observance is the theme of "vocation." The choice of vocation or occupation in the modern world seems far more closely oriented to income possibilities than to accepting the kind of work that would enable the individual Christian and the entire work force to glorify God in an unqualified way through that work. The church is almost silent today in challenging members, especially the young, to think seriously about vocational choice. Alert youth advisors, Sunday school teachers, church sessions, and pastors consistently seek to help able and qualified young people to discern a possible call of God to positions of leadership in the church first before young people seriously consider other kinds of work.

Leith makes a salient point about the way in which our tradition regards the divine majesty. "More than a century ago Alexander Schweizer observed that Calvinism is distinguished from Lutheranism by its emphasis on the majesty of God and by its assault on all forms of paganism in the medieval church, whereas Lutheranism had been primarily concerned with 'judaistic' lapses into salvation by works."[9] It is quite possible that some aspects of the Reformed tradition are related to this concern about idolatry in worship. Instead of the church pageantry, the flowing garments worn by high church officials in the Roman Church, the veneration of relics, and the bowing and scraping accorded church leaders, the Reformers taught simplicity in worship, modesty in dress, and what came to be an austere demeanor as evidenced by those reformers we know as the Pilgrims. Presbyterians are now breaking that mold.

In speaking about the manner in which Presbyterians confess our relation to God, we say that each adopted creed or confession of the church must be seen in its context. We more or less understand that many of the matters discussed in that creed are particularly relevant to the age or situation in which the confession was written. In a similar manner, it is essential that we review what the ecclesiastical milieu was for the actions and written documents of Luther and Calvin. Specifically, those two great Reformers were giving new guidance and stating their convictions in opposition to church practices of the sixteenth century.

John Calvin wrote that "the testimony of the Spirit is superior to all reason. For as God alone is sufficient witness of himself [sic] in his own word, so also the word will never gain credit in the hearts of men [sic], till it be confirmed by the internal testimony of the Spirit."[10] This reference to the work of the Spirit in scripture returns us to the major Reformation emphases upon the Holy Spirit and scripture. At Pentecost the Spirit descended upon the followers of Jesus *assembled* (Acts 2:1). At Antioch the followers were *gathered* worshiping and fasting when the Spirit called the church to set apart Paul and Barnabas for mission work (Acts 13:2). The Spirit also worked in and through individuals, but whenever the (Presbyterian) church gathers, it seeks to discern the will of God as revealed through God's Spirit.

The Reformation principle that the church is always reforming has an implication that is not always accepted in fact. That implication is that the church, led by the Spirit, is always open to new revelation and to fresh expressions of old truths. In practice, the church should never fear "new theologies"; therefore, newer insights and emphases are not to be rejected out of hand, but are to be studied, pondered, and considered for possible inclusion in one's own theological formulations, as well as in the corporate theological statements of the church. The Holy Spirit is alive!

In our time we have been almost literally bombarded with new perspectives, but the true Reformed Christian must reject the initial impulse to cast aside as being unworthy those doctrines or propositions previously unknown to Reformed theology. Illustrations abound. We have necessarily become more than casually acquainted with feminist theology, liberation theology, process theology, and black theology, for instance, and increasingly, we anticipate, we will be confronted with various Third World theologies. We in the mainline churches should rejoice as we encourage indigenous hymnody among churches in the developing world, as those hymns express a theology that may be just developing as it is sung, perhaps not yet fully mature, according to our perspective.

Once again the contemporary Presbyterian Church (U.S.A.) as a whole finds itself amazingly in tune with its scattered parts on the key elements and heritage of Reformed theology. This state of affairs is a cause for celebration. We can sing, in the words of John Calvin:

> I greet Thee, who my sure Redeemer art,
> My only trust and Savior of my heart,
> Who pain didst undergo for my poor sake;
> I pray Thee from our hearts all cares to take.
>
> . . . .
>
> Thou art the life, by which alone we live,
> And all our substance and our strength receive;
> Sustain us by Thy faith and by Thy power,
> And give us strength in every trying hour.
>
> Thou hast the true and perfect gentleness,
> No harshness hast Thou and no bitterness:
> O grant to us the grace we find in Thee,
> That we may dwell in perfect unity.

Our hope is in no other save in Thee;
Our faith is built upon Thy promise free;
Lord, give us peace, and make us calm and sure,
That in Thy strength we evermore endure.[11]

Calvin's theology permeates this hymn. The first stanza echoes the theme of Christ as Redeemer and Savior who suffered for humanity. Our strength, in the second stanza, comes from the model for our lives in Christ who sustains us. Jesus was divine man who was gentle, with no harshness or bitterness and who was full of grace. The human's hope is only in Christ, who grants peace, serenity, and endurance. God is the sovereign creator and redeemer. Praise be to God!

3

Witherspoon Is Not Just a Street Name in Louisville, KY

Our Constitutional Heritage

"Preliminary Principles" in the *Book of Order*

Is an expert chef one who always uses a recipe, or one who either knows the recipe so well that a recipe is not needed or who understands ingredients sufficiently that a recipe is not required? Is a rule book necessary for bridge or for parliamentary procedure? How important is "the book" the day before an examination for a driver's license? One answer only may not be satisfactory for the above questions, but surprisingly, some so-called rule books can be quite different from what was anticipated. We should never forget John Witherspoon. President of the College of New Jersey (now Princeton University), he was the only minister to sign the Declaration of Independence. He was the person primarily responsible for calling into being the first General Assembly in 1789, and he served as its presiding officer until John Rogers was elected the first moderator of the General Assembly. Witherspoon was instrumental in launching the constitutional heritage of American Presbyterianism.

In the Presbyterian Church (U.S.A.), the first four chapters in the *Book of Order*[1]—which is one half of the rule book, our *Constitution*—suggest a kind of "Aha!" experience. They are far different and far more than just rules. "The *Book of Order* is *not* a manual of operations. It is a way of making Christian life in community possible."[2] These chapters provide a vision for the church.

Mission and unity are described *first*, and within that framework of purpose and intent, the rules follow. We are often joking when we say that Presbyterians do things decently and in order, but polity, our form of government, is one thing that unites us. Polity, however, follows other more essential "corporate glue." These chapters of the *Book of Order* provide a richness with sometimes lilting language and profound thoughts, showing us our fundamental unity in (1) acknowledging Jesus Christ as living Lord, (2) the centrality of the Bible, and (3) our *Book of Confessions*. Then comes polity or our form of governance.

The Head of the Church

Presbyterians are united in the unequivocal, magnificent phrases in chapter I of the *Book of Order* (Form of Government): "All power in heaven and earth is given to Jesus Christ by Almighty God, who raised Christ from the dead and set him above all rule and authority, all power and dominion, and every name that is named, not only in this age but also in that which is to come. God has put all things under the Lordship[3] of Jesus Christ and has made Christ Head of the Church, which is his body" (G-1.0100a).

Some early church creeds begin with a discussion of the Bible, but both the Confession of 1967 and the still newer Brief Statement of Faith, both in our *Book of Confessions*, start with the center of our faith, Jesus Christ—in a manner strongly approved by our church. If this initial paragraph sounds reminiscent of Paul's letter to the church in Ephesus, it should. Ephesians 1:20, for instance, states, "God put this power to work when he raised him from the dead and seated him at his right hand in the heavenly places." The great hymn that closes chapter 1 in this book uses another figure, speaking of the church as the bride of Christ, an intimate and compelling image, joining the figure of speech here of the church as the body of Christ. It is very clear that the aim of everything that follows in the *Book of Order* and everything in the church is to recognize Jesus as the great Head of the church.

This section then states that Christ "calls the church into being, giving it all that is necessary for its mission to the world, with the undergirding promise of being present with the church." We sometimes stumble trying to figure who should lead what in the church, but the assurance here is that Christ alone rules, teaches, calls, and uses the church. Harried church leaders can relax a bit, and church members need not be unduly anxious simply because the ultimate rule of the church is not with us, but with Christ.

The recurring theme, already noted in the introduction to this book, of Jesus praying for unity in the church is struck here again: "Christ gives to his church its faith and life, its unity and mission, its officers and ordinances." The Spirit of God provides guidance, and we are to use sound judgment, following the clear teachings of scripture, when subjects have been treated in the Bible.

"The Church confesses that he is its hope and that the church, as Christ's body, is bound to his authority and thus free to live in the lively, joyous reality of the grace of God." Some of our ancestors were pretty strong on an almost joyless faith, but that is certainly not the note sounded here. Let it be underscored and written in bold type that at the very beginning **Presbyterians are united in their basic and primary commitment to God in Jesus Christ**. In discussions and debates on a variety of issues it is essential that we convey to others what we would insist upon for ourselves: our belief in and commitment to the ringing language that **Jesus Christ is Head of the church**.

In discussing the last paragraph in the Apostles' Creed about the church as "the communion of saints," John Calvin links the notion of salvation with God's purposes in establishing the church. He notes that since the church is composed of those elected by God, the church cannot fail, quoting Psalm 46:5, "God is in the midst of the city [Zion]; it cannot be moved." Individual redemption is thus tied to God's eternal purposes for the church, the holy community, and it is done for God's glory.[4]

James H. Smylie has put it this way: "In the Reformed view

of the church, God calls the Christian community into being through the work of Christ and the Holy Spirit. The church is a community of faith and life that is called to share Christ's story with the world. As such, Christians belong to a communion of saints, not a hierarchical order in heaven but a community of the dead and the living, the number of which is known only to God."[5]

Over and over again the necessary relation between salvation and service is stressed by the Reformed tradition. The Heidelberg Catechism ties these two vital aspects of the Christian faith in one question and answer:

> Q. What is your only comfort, in life and in death?
> A. That I belong—body and soul, in life and in death—
> not to myself but to my faithful Savior, Jesus Christ. . . .
> Therefore, by his Holy Spirit, he also assures me of eternal life, and makes me wholeheartedly willing and ready from now on to live for him.[6]

Even a casual reading of the early chapters of 1 Corinthians is sufficient for us to accept the fact that the church has been imperfect in all ages as the apostle Paul details the horrible sins of the community of faith in Corinth. Even when one believes that there are failings in the Presbyterian Church today, it is instructive to continue to believe that the church is an institution created by God in Jesus Christ.

The specific affirmations in chapter I of the *Book of Order* (Form of Government) under "The Head of the Church" are daunting. Christ, it says,

> Calls the church into being
> Gives the church its faith and life
> Is the church's authority

Christ gives the church "all that is necessary for its mission to the world, for its building up, and for its service to God." For the moment our concentration is on the "building up," noting that the language is not for its tearing down or its destruction. If, in fact, the church has been given all that is necessary by its founder for building up, is it not appropriate for each church member, and especially for each church leader, to be searching for ways this branch of the whole church may be built up?

Further, if the church has been given all that is necessary for its mission, it is a labor-intensive task to discern what mission is being given to this church in our time. Suffice it to say that, once again, there is concurrence among Presbyterians that God has given us a mission, even when we have not yet fully agreed upon its detailed dimensions and directions.

It is worth noting in this section that Christ uses the "ministry of women and men" in exercising his authority. Since Jesus himself said, "Let anyone among you who is without sin be the first to throw a stone at her" (John 8:7), and then, "Go your way, and from now on do not sin again" (John 8:11), we would have a terrible burden in desiring to read others out of the church, particularly when we have a growing understanding that we agree on the foundations of the church. The object of purity is to be commended, but we must always be asking, "How is Christ forgiving us now?" and "How most carefully do we administer the authority given to us?"

In times of stress and strain in the Christian fellowship we should meet neighbors in the faith, not as antagonists, but as others who share the good news of Jesus Christ so that it is not only all right, but essential for us to share mutually through our expressions of "lively joy" when we are together or live apart.

The Great Ends of the Church

Church union has often been the occasion for new insights, understandings, and celebrations. Already well established in the United Presbyterian Church of North America from its adoption early in the twentieth century, this section was a beautiful gift to the union in 1958 with the Presbyterian Church in the U.S.A., and later to the union of those two branches with the Presbyterian Church in the United States in 1983. This "Great Ends" statement is so significant that the six General Assembly agencies are proposing that the Great Ends be emphasized throughout the church as we begin a new millennium, and that they be the theme for General Assembly meetings from 1998 to 2003.

> The great ends of the church are the proclamation of the gospel for the salvation of humankind; the shelter, nurture, and spiritual fellowship of the children of God; the maintenance of divine worship; the preservation of the truth; the promotion of social righteousness; and the exhibition of the Kingdom of Heaven to the world.
>
> (G-1.0200)

1. **". . . the proclamation of the gospel for the salvation of humankind."** There is nothing about which Presbyterians say they agree more than outreach and witness to the nation, and all nations. Researchers have confirmed that the primary reasons for a drop in membership in the Presbyterian Church in recent years have been threefold: (1) new church development has slowed; (2) Presbyterians have not produced sufficient offspring—the children of members have been the most significant reason for church growth, historically, in this country, and we have lost youth and others who have not returned to the church; and (3) the United States is increasingly a racial ethnic nation, but the Presbyterian Church (U.S.A.) is predominantly white Anglo-Saxon.[7] Surely, the time has come for Presbyterians to turn old patterns around to reach out and to share the good news of God's love in Christ.

The sometimes unstated fact is that the Presbyterian Church has not changed its historic pattern of not being very vocal about telling others about Christ. That is not new. What *is* a recent development is that at a time when the church was losing members for other reasons, outreach and mission were insufficient to maintain the size of the body of believers *in this country.* It is fascinating that a number of the partner churches around the world that were established, humanly speaking, through the missionary efforts of American Presbyterians have taken to heart and practiced much more effectively what the American Presbyterians have said about witness and evangelism. There are, for instance, more Presbyterians in Korea than there are in the United States!

2. ". . . the shelter, nurture, and spiritual fellowship of the children of God." Unanimity of acceptance of this statement must also be close to universal in the Presbyterian family. Without taking a scientific poll, a judgment is that Presbyterians feel that they have done a fairly good job of implementing this statement. Pastoral care and the nurture of the faithful are essential. Governing bodies are seeking anew to provide resources and nurture for congregations, and that is most encouraging in and of itself, as well as also in binding us together. In new and creative ways the Christian Education Program Area of the Congregational Ministries Division of the General Assembly Council is seeking to resource congregations even more effectively in curriculum materials, and in other resources and aids for insuring opportunities for growth and nurture in every aspect of the life of the congregation.

If "shelter" is taken literally, few can question the dedication of Presbyterians to both erecting and maintaining in good shape places for worship and nurture. Since many church members are realtors, architects, contractors, and skilled craftspeople by profession, it is not surprising that church buildings are often aesthetically pleasing, well-constructed, and kept in good repair.

3. ". . . the maintenance of divine worship." Unfortunately, the "Directory for Worship" in the Book of Order is much less well known and used than the "Form of Government" section, but on the other hand, it is mercifully better known than the section called "The Rules of Discipline"! To whet our appetite for a fuller consideration of worship in a later chapter we can remind ourselves that we deeply confess our faith in worship in ways other than reciting a formal confession of faith. James L. Mays's treatment of the familiar Psalm 100 clearly indicates that what we say about God in worship can be a tremendous

political statement as well as indicating *social action*. Mays says, "Worship that names God is the confession of *one* God."[8] That clearly means that we will have no other gods, and that is precisely what the Reformed church in Germany proclaimed in the Declaration of Barmen, contained in our *Book of Confessions*. The church would worship God, and not bow to Hitler! In this psalm "come into the presence" and "serve" are clear references to a king. There are symbols and rituals here from political life so that when we opt in worship for one "power structure"—God over king—we are taking "the most significant social action that people can take."[9] The "maintenance of divine worship" is, of course, worship of the divine, whom we call God.

The opening paragraph in the "Directory for Worship" is most appropriate: "This Directory for Worship reflects the conviction that the life of the Church is one, and that its worship, witness, and service are inseparable. . . . A Directory for Worship is not a service book with fixed orders of worship, a collection of prayers and rituals, or a program guide. Rather it describes the theology that underlies Reformed worship and outlines appropriate forms for that worship."[10]

4. ". . . the preservation of truth." "Theology matters!" was the ringing declaration of Presbyterians at the 206th General Assembly (1994) following prolonged discussion across the church about Reformed theology and related issues. Truth, honesty, and integrity seem to be casualties in much of modern life, but the Presbyterian Church can be a harbinger of things to come insofar as its discussions, arguments, debates and writings are based on truth. Open and honest differences of opinion are to be tolerated—yes, even encouraged—but distortions of the truth are not. Reformed theology was discussed in the previous chapter, and the creeds will be considered in the next chapter.

5. ". . . the promotion of social righteousness." The impression is often left that social justice issues originated with the social gospel in the early part of the twentieth century, and that the "promotion of social righteousness" was a foreign concept to the Christian church. The footnote in the *Book of Order* states that this entire paragraph was adopted by the United Presbyterian Church of North America in 1910.

It is so easy, somehow, to ignore the prophetic books of the Old Testament, to say nothing about Jesus' statement of his mission at Nazareth, as recorded in the fourth chapter of Luke, a quotation from Isaiah 61:1, 2a: "The spirit of the Lord GOD is upon me, because the LORD has anointed me; he has sent me to bring good news to the oppressed, to bind up the brokenhearted, to proclaim liberty to the captives, and release to the prisoners; to proclaim the year of the LORD's favor." That was written long before 1900.

Defense of the status quo, particularly as it affects "my" position in the world, has seemed to outweigh social justice concerns raised by the less fortunate in worldly terms, especially when I may have to give up some cherished possession or position for there to be true justice. Note, again, the wording. It is not even the "practice" of social justice that is called for, but the "promotion" of social righteousness.

Membership gain or loss is not the chief concern of the church; faithful, balanced witness is. Such faithfulness must combine the zeal of a determined effort to make Christ known, with an equal determination to live out the tough choices related to peace, social justice, inclusiveness, and acceptance regardless of race, language, gender, position, or power—or lack thereof. It is far too tempting to talk about the "spiritual" aspects of the Christian life while ignoring the brash and thundering words of the prophets of the Old Testament and the clear teachings of Jesus.

In the seventh volume of the Presbyterian Presence series, Milton J Coalter, John M. Mulder, and Louis B. Weeks wrote, "Virtually every issue that consumes the attention of late twentieth-century Presbyterians and mainstream Protestants was addressed in religious reform movements of the early nineteenth century—war, racism, economic justice, substance abuse (principally alcohol), feminism, urban blight, crime, prison reform, and others."[11]

In fact, both "conservative evangelicals" and "liberals" in the various Presbyterian streams have been far more united in social justice and human rights issues than has sometimes been recognized, coming together particularly on peace issues in recent years. "The first official pronouncement on slavery by the Presbyterian Church's highest judicatory was in 1787."[12] At the first meeting of the new United Presbyterian Church of North America in 1858 an action in opposition to slavery was taken.[13] Presbyterian Church in the United States missionary to China Hampden DuBose "fought vigorously against the opium trade."[14] A Presbyterian businessman wrote *New Themes for the Protestant Clergy* in 1854, about the church's "failure to denounce contemporary covetousness as sin."[15] In 1953, John Mackay, moderator of the Presbyterian Church in the U.S.A., wrote a "Letter to Presbyterians" opposing the anticommunist hysteria of McCarthyism, including action endorsed by the General Council and the General Assembly.[16] Happily, persons of all theological positions today understand the necessity to address corporate—as well as individual—sin.

6. "... and the exhibition of the Kingdom of Heaven to the world." This is a difficult one in at least two ways, but we pose a way out of any dilemma. First, who knows precisely what the kingdom of heaven is? (The term "kingdom of heaven" in Matthew seems to be the same as "kingdom of God" in the other Gospels. The familiar "Thy kingdom come" in the Lord's Prayer is the King James Version of Matthew 6:10). Donald K. McKim defines the kingdom of heaven as "God's sovereign reign and rule. God's reign was the major focus of Jesus' teaching. . . . Its fullness is in the future . . . and yet it has also come in Jesus himself."[17] The "Great Ends of the Church" phrase, in this context, written in 1910, probably meant for the Christian (and the church, collectively) to live in a godlike manner.

That brings us to the second tough part: living, or "exhibiting" a life that is as near to perfection as possible, a Christlike life. All of us Calvinists know that we are sinful creatures, and that we will never adequately represent the God of steadfast love to exhibit the kind of God we know, but our hope is this: that despite any poor representations we make, God's witness to God's own self can still be made in ways which pass all understanding. God will be praised, and we will bask in the sure knowledge of a forgiving God of mercy and grace.

All of this comes together in chapter III of the *Book of Order*, "The Church and Its Mission." The language there reads, "The Church of Jesus Christ is the provisional demonstration of what God intends for all of humanity" (G-3.0200). The statements of the ideal are that the church is "called to be a sign in and for the world . . . , the new humanity, a new creation, a new beginning for human life," wherein "Sin is forgiven. Reconciliation is accomplished. The dividing walls of hostility are torn down" (G-3.0200a–b). To whatever extent the "provisional demonstration" is realized, the church "exhibits the Kingdom of Heaven."

The Historic Principles
of Church Order

The footnote in the *Book of Order* for this section (G-1.0300) never ceases to amaze those who see it for the first time. Except for the first paragraph, the section was adopted in 1788 and set the tone for open and honest differences of opinion and conviction within the framework of a constitutional system of church government.

1. "That 'God alone is Lord of the conscience, and hath left it free from the doctrines and commandments of men[18] which are in anything contrary to his Word, or beside it, in matters of faith or worship.'" Few sections of the entire *Book of Order* are more frequently quoted or noted than this section (quoted in turn from the Westminster Confession). It forms the basis for disagreement, dissent, and disputation, since the possibility of free conviction and expression in the church hang upon it. *"God alone is Lord of the conscience."* With tolerance and respect within prescribed strictures, the majority is constrained to hear the minority, even if it is a minority of one.

Without casting aspersions on any other form of civil or church government, it can be said that Presbyterian polity allows for open dissent. One needs to trace history no further back than the struggles of Martin Luther to view the stark contrast here to such things as the teaching about the infallibility of the pope in certain situations in the Roman Catholic Church. In all candor, theology, worship, and such things as biblical interpretation aside, these words of democratic intent stake out a position that has been tested by time within the Presbyterian family worldwide, and is the envy of many who serve under hierarchical forms of ecclesiastical or civil government.

2. The next paragraph accentuates **the rights of private judgment in religious matters as universal and unalienable.** It goes on to state boldly that the religious constituencies should not be aided by a civil power—the strong doctrine of the separation of church and state. Among other things, this is a ringing declaration for one of the longest words in the English language, disestablishmentarianism, that is, that no church should be the official or established religion of the country. In affirmative language, the church shall be free of the state. From our perspective of well over two hundred years in time, and of never having had a state religion, it is difficult to comprehend how radical this doctrine was when it was promulgated. Virtually all settlers in the United States in the first hundred and fifty years had come from a country where religion had been established. Denominations were created first in the United States! In the *Book of Confessions*, the Theological Declaration of Barmen, adopted by the Reformed church in Germany under Hitler in May 1934, is a twentieth-century reaffirmation of the principle that the state must not exercise control of religion.

3. Here it is stated **that any church is free to adopt its own terms of membership, and that "our blessed Savior, for the edification of the visible Church, which is his body," has appointed officers to preach the gospel, administer the sacraments, and exercise discipline for the preservation of truth.** This is another one of the generally accepted tenets of Presby-

terians, although it must be noted that on occasion there can be a decided difference about what those entrance terms should be for church membership, and especially about the qualifications of those chosen for leadership. Although there is almost unanimity across the denomination in how sessions actually accept new members, the principle of "local option" is in effect so that each session can set its own standards for "admission into its communion," or membership into that church fellowship.

It is true, of course, that all admission standards must fall within constitutional boundaries, and if problems arise, any appeal of any kind would go through the church's legal system, Part III of the *Book of Order*, "The Rules of Discipline."

4. The qualification that governing bodies "may . . . err" is significant as it tempers those who otherwise might believe they are "all-wise." A dash of humility is often just what all kinds of leaders need. Further, **"no church governing body ought to pretend to make laws to bind the conscience."** If a church is "always reforming," it is reforming from some perceived past error. The principle is clear: This church admits it is not perfect, so no member or officer should be unduly dogmatic.

The Historic Principles of Church Government

Most of the issues that bring us together in governing bodies are discussed in the special chapter on polity, but several points mentioned under this heading in chapter I of the *Book of Order* should be noted here. All of the congregations together form one church of Christ, and the larger part of the church— we usually say the higher governing body—should govern a smaller, or determine matters of controversy. In fact, in practice there is sometimes a healthy tension between the presbyteries and the General Assembly at this point. Next, and very important, is that a majority should govern, and that may on occasion mean a 99–98 vote, for example. Then it is noted that appeals may be handed from a lower governing body to a higher body until ultimately a decision is reached. Finally, the principles and procedures on church government are drawn from "the primitive church," what we normally refer to as the early church, in the Bible.

The Constitution Defined

The Constitution is composed of two parts: the *Book of Confessions* and the *Book of Order*. The *Book of Confessions* consists of the Nicene Creed, the Apostles' Creed, the Scots Confession, the Heidelberg Catechism, the Second Helvetic Confession, the Westminster Confession of Faith, the Shorter Catechism, the Larger Catechism, the Theological Declaration of Barmen, the Confession of 1967, and A Brief Statement of Faith—Presbyterian Church (U.S.A.).

The *Book of Order* includes the Form of Government, the Directory for Worship, and the Rules of Discipline.

The Presbyterian bonds are deep and meaningful. Our serving under the Lordship of Jesus Christ is preeminent. The Great Ends of the Church are emblematic of a rounded and balanced church seeking to be faithful in worship, nurture, and service. The Historic Principles of Church Order and Church Government are relevant to today's ever-changing world because we state emphatically that we are ever reforming. Our renewal and reformation demand that we struggle hard at changing as we may need, as we rush enthusiastically into the third millennium.

> For all the saints who from their labors rest,
> Who Thee by faith before the world confessed,
> Thy name, O Jesus, be forever blest.
> Alleluia! Alleluia!
>
> . . . .
>
> O blest communion, fellowship divine!
> We feebly struggle, they in glory shine;
> Yet all are one in Thee, for all are Thine.
> Alleluia! Alleluia!

From earth's wide bounds, from ocean's farthest coast,
Through gates of pearl streams in the countless host,
Singing to Father, Son and Holy Ghost,
Alleluia! Alleluia!

(William Walsham How)[19]

4

When We Say, "We Believe . . ."
The Church and Its Confessions

One pastor of a 2,500-member church has, we are told, the annoying and magnificent custom, after opening weekly staff meetings with a Bible reading and reflection on it, of then insisting that each staff person commit herself or himself to a stance on the biblical material. No one can escape from staking out a position or taking a stand on the issue of the week! Our denomination has taken its stand on the *Book of Confessions*.[1]

A Confessional Church

The Presbyterian Church (U.S.A.) is a confessional church, defining who we are and what we believe. While others turn to a bishop for identifying where the church stands, and still others forcefully state that they have no creed other than the Bible, we have a formal confession or belief, or really a series of confessions. A confession (*confessio*—profession of faith) or a creed (*credo*—I believe) is a statement of beliefs or convictions. A new immigrant to the United States who becomes a citizen swears to uphold the Constitution, and the ceremony is a time of joy and celebration. With their hands held high, the new citizens often cry in happiness at their testimony. It is a moment of commitment; and so it is when a citizen of the church proudly and enthusiastically announces: Here I stand; I accept Christ as Lord, and this is what I humbly and movingly believe.

A Book of Confessions

The *Book of Confessions* is comprised of two ancient creeds from the early church: the Apostles' Creed and the Nicene Creed. Six come from the Reformation period: the Scots Confession; the Heidelberg Catechism; the Second Helvetic Confession; and three written by a group of Puritan clergymen of the Church of England—often called the Westminster divines—between 1643 and 1649 at Westminster Abbey in London, the Westminster Confession, the Westminster Larger Catechism, and the Westminster Shorter Catechism. Three are modern creeds: the Theological Declaration of Barmen from the Nazi era in Germany, the Confession of 1967, and A Brief Statement of Faith—Presbyterian Church (U.S.A.).[2]

In *Presbyterian Creeds: A Guide to The Book of Confessions*, Jack Rogers has provided the church with a helpful summary of what the *Book of Order* says about the theological content of these creeds.

> The *Book of Order* . . . [lists] ten doctrines which we can take to be essential and necessary. Two are noted as shared with the church catholic, or universal: the mystery of the Trinity, and the incarnation of the eternal Word of God in Jesus Christ. Two are identified with our affirmation of the Protestant Reformation: justification by grace through faith, and Scripture as the final authority for salvation and the life of faith. . . . The six themes . . . characteristic of the Reformed tradition are God's sovereignty; God's choosing (election) of people for salvation and service; the covenant life of the church, ordering itself according to the Word of God; a faithful stewardship of God's creation; the sin of idolatry, which makes anything created ultimate, rather than worshipping only the Creator; and the necessity of obedience to the Word of God, which directs us to work for justice in the transformation of society.[3]

Most creeds or confessions have been adopted at a time of crisis, or to settle or conclude an ongoing theological debate within the life of the church. The two most recent confessions in the Presbyterian Church (U.S.A.) *Book of Confessions* have a different history. Each was prepared following a Presbyterian union. At the 170th General Assembly (1958) in Pittsburgh when the United Presbyterian Church of North America and the Presbyterian Church in the United States of America merged, a Special Committee was chosen to write a contemporary confession for the "new" denomination. After much research, discussion, writing and rewriting over a period of years, the Confession of 1967 was adopted in Portland, Oregon, at the 179th General Assembly (1967).[4]

The Special Committee that made the initial draft of what became the Confession of 1967 also made an innovative proposal: that the church adopt a book of confessions. Only the Westminster Confession of Faith and the Westminster Larger and Shorter Catechisms had historically been the confessional documents of Presbyterians in this country. The task of having the new Confession of 1967 adopted by the church was probably made easier by not substituting it for the Westminster Confession, but by adding other historic creeds in addition to the proposed new confession, and by retaining the Westminster documents (except for the little-used Larger Catechism).

At the time of the reunion of the United Presbyterian Church in the U.S.A. and the Presbyterian Church in the United States in 1983, the entire *Book of Confessions* was adopted by the reunited church. Following that reunion a committee was chosen that drafted a document which survived the constitutional process with flying colors and became A Brief Statement of Faith, which was adopted in 1991.

How does all of this relate to the subject at hand?

1. The Church Believes
That Forming Creeds Brings Us Together

The *Book of Confessions*, including now A Brief Statement of Faith, has been through the crucible of having been tested by fire. That is, the entire church has thoroughly reviewed and discussed this portion of the *Constitution*, and it has been enthusiastically approved. The *Book of Confessions* is a linchpin that holds the church together as one General Assembly and one church. Theological unity on a wide range of subjects is probably impossible, but a concurrence on the essence of the faith in the Reformed tradition is not just possible; it has been done. Those holding a wide spectrum of theological convictions *can* discuss their differences in openness and in integrity with mutual respect. Learning to listen and learning how to resolve conflicts are lessons in process.

Those who have the determination to keep the church together may learn something by the very process that brought A Brief Statement to the church. Jack Rogers writes, "It may be the first time in the history of Reformed creedal formation that a group was chosen specifically for its diversity and then expected to write a document evoking unity." Of the twenty-one women and men there were people from a broad theological perspective with a variety of gifts and experiences; different racial-ethnic groups were represented; members of the Committee included older and younger persons, church members, church officers, and ministers.[5]

2. The Confessions Not Only Unite the Presbyterian Church (U.S.A.); They Also Unite Us with the Whole Church of Jesus Christ

These creeds especially tie us to the Reformed family of churches. Although the Christian church is expanding rapidly in some parts of the world, notably in Africa and China, there is almost a "hunkering-down" mentality for members of the mainline churches in the United States; each has lost members in recent years. It is particularly propitious at this time to be reminded of our heritage and of our participation with other Christians in a worldwide fellowship of believers. We can gain encouragement and support from them as we watch how they address the issues that confront them socially and economically, as well as theologically and biblically.

The Ancient Creeds

Theological disagreements are not new, to make the understatement of the decade. Rigorous debate and serious discussions can help us all to grow, and particularly if we discuss reasonably and calmly, some new measure of respect may be gained from those with whom we may disagree, and some new light may dawn. As noted earlier, creedal formation has often come from an effort to settle disputes about truth. That was certainly the case of the oldest creed in our *Book of Confessions*.

1. The Nicene Creed

This is our oldest creed, and it came about because the Emperor Constantine wanted peace in the church as devout persons struggled to articulate their faith. So he called the Council of Nicaea in A.D. 325 (Nicaea is on a little lake in Asiatic Turkey, near the Sea of Marmara). The principal issue revolved around the nature of Jesus. Was he human—maybe a prophet or even some kind of magician? Was he divine—perhaps an angel? The nature of the problem has been stated this way:

> [T]he Christ to whom faith responds is the Christ who is presented in the *kerygma* [proclamation], and that is the exalted Christ, the living and present Lord. But this Christ cannot be divorced from the Christ who occupied a place on the stage of history, who lived and died and was raised again by God. Faith must . . . bring the dimension of historical depth into the picture of the kerygmatic Christ; it must unite the Christ who is present in the Spirit with the Christ who suffered in the flesh.[6]

Although not finally approved until the meeting of another worldwide council, the Council of Chalcedon (in modern Asiatic Turkey across the Bosporus from Istanbul) in A.D. 451, the basic understanding reached at Nicaea became accepted. The operative language is somewhat arcane for us, but it becomes clear when we recognize the style of writing. The second section, in part, is,

> We believe . . . in one Lord Jesus Christ, the only-begotten Son of God, begotten of the Father before all worlds, God of God, Light of Light, Very God of Very God, begotten, not made, being of one substance with the Father, by whom all things were made; who for us men [sic], and for our salvation, came down from heaven, and was incarnate by the Holy Spirit of the Virgin Mary, and was made man, and was crucified also for us under Pontius Pilate.

"God of God" and "Very God of Very God" mean that absolutely without a doubt Jesus was God, and for those fourth- and fifth-century Christians a key word in Greek was "of one substance," that is, being completely and fully God. John 1:1 is helpful for us: "In the beginning was the Word, and the Word was with God, and the Word was God" when we understand "the Word" to refer to Jesus. The part that identifies Jesus as being human, also, is stated in such phrases as "came down from heaven, and was incarnate," and it goes on to say that "he suffered, was buried," all to emphasize the true humanity of Jesus.

Thus, the Nicene Creed tells us unequivocally that Jesus was both God and human. Birthed to resolve controversy, this creed has served its purpose magnificently. There is one other comment about this creed which needs to be recorded. The Nicene is the only creed fully recognized by the church in the West and the church in the East, that is, by the Roman Catholic and Protestant churches in the West and the Orthodox churches in the East. When the World Council of Churches meets, this is the one creed that is familiar to and accepted by all.

2. The Apostles' Creed

It needs to be said, first, that the Apostles' Creed is not properly named—it does not come from the early Apostles—but it *is* correctly named in that it accurately reflects the teachings and the beliefs of Christians from very early times. Eastern Christians in the Orthodox churches have no early records of this creed as being historic and by "the Apostles," but the nucleus of this creed is certainly ancient.

In the Presbyterian Church this creed is extremely well known and used regularly in worship. Like the Nicene Creed, the Apostles' Creed is trinitarian as it develops around the three persons of the godhead: Father, Son, and Holy Ghost (Spirit). The Gloria, regularly used in Presbyterian worship until recent years, obviously uses this formula. Its roots are clearly discernible in Matthew 28:19–20: "Go therefore and make disciples of all nations, baptizing them in the name of the Father and of the Son and of the Holy Spirit, and teaching them . . . " John Calvin's *Institutes of the Christian Religion* were written to help in understanding this creed, the Lord's Prayer, and the Ten Commandments, so it is no wonder that the Creed, the Prayer, and the Ten Commandments have been so vital in the history and life of Presbyterians.

The Creeds of the
Reformation Period

The Committee on Biblical Authority and Interpretation which reported to the 194th General Assembly (1982) of the United Presbyterian Church in the U.S.A. stated, in part:

The sixteenth and seventeenth century Reformed theological confessions, adopted in the Book of Confessions, evidence three characteristics of this developmental period. First, our confessions are catholic, acknowledging their agreement with the ancient creeds affirmed by the church universal. Second, the Reformed confessions are Protestant, affirming that the church must be reformed, and ever reforming, according to the word of God attested in canonical Scripture. Third, these confessions are evangelical, recognizing the centrality of the gospel of Jesus Christ as the life-renewing and culture-shaping power of God that continually creates and sustains the church in its ministry and mission to the world.[7]

As we shall see, not only was the Scots Confession written in a political "moment" of high tension and high stakes, but the Heidelberg Catechism became the center of controversy at a time when Frederick III, elector of the Palatinate, could have been expelled from his post. The social and justice issues surrounding these creeds were vitally important. We are united today on political involvement, social justice, and human rights causes as our understanding from the Bible demands it, *but also* because our creedal formulations will not permit our ignoring such issues. We also recognize the powerful political problem at the time of the Theological Declaration of Barmen, but the opening sentence of the Scots Confession is of the same genre: "We confess and acknowledge one God alone. . . ." No political power in London should sway the Scottish Parliament!

1. *The Scots Confession*

Composed by John Knox and five others in 1560 in four days, the Scots Confession was, in a very real sense, a political document, because it was written for the Scottish Parliament to be enacted at a time when Scotland might have become Roman Catholic. Like the Apostles' Creed, "The Scots Confession was written about basic beliefs concerning the Father, the Son and the Holy Spirit, with two additions, on the church and on the consummation," as Edward A. Dowey has outlined it.[8] This confession has been fundamental for Presbyterian bodies worldwide, in addition to being the foundational creed for the Church of Scotland.

2. *The Heidelberg Catechism*

A different structure has been used for the Heidelberg Catechism, since there is one question and one or more answers for each Lord's Day of the year, so it has been readily adaptable for Sunday school classes. Also written at a time of political and ecclesiastical high tension, the catechism was well-known to the Reformed Church in Germany at the time when Hitler wanted conformity to the state church, but those who wrote and voted for the Barmen Declaration knew of the courage and conviction inherent in this catechism. The catechism "was written in three main sections. The first dealt with sin and guilt. The second and longest part discussed redemption and freedom. The final section treated thankfulness to God in obedience and prayer."[9]

3. The Second Helvetic Confession

Heinrich Bullinger was successor to Huldrych Zwingli after Zwingli was killed. As pastor of the magnificent Great Münster Church in Zurich, Bullinger wrote the Second Helvetic Confession in 1561. The Münster Church is still located at the center of social life in Zurich, and it was there that Zwingli abolished the Lenten fast and insisted upon the spiritual nature of the Lord's Supper, and that the Mass was not the actual breaking of the body and drinking of the blood of Christ. Bullinger had lived the Reformation period, and in an effort to assist those who supported the Reformation in Europe, particularly the Elector Frederick of the German province of the Palatinate, he wrote this confession. The confession contains thirty chapters, "divided between two major sections: the first on theology and the second on the church, ministry, and sacraments,"[10] the latter incorporating the earlier teaching of Zwingli. Significantly, chapter II in this confession is about the interpretation of scripture—another section that helps unite Presbyterians today!

4. The Westminster Confession,
with the Larger and Shorter Catechisms of 1647

Until 1967 these were the sole confessional documents of Presbyterians in this country, the theological glue that held the church together. Of course, the Westminster Assembly was, in one sense, not a church gathering at all, but an Assembly called together by the English Parliament. In 1649, before it

finished its work (it never adjourned!), a king had been be-
headed, as had the Archbishop of Canterbury, and Oliver
Cromwell was in charge. It was also a revolutionary period—
our creeds seem to have evolved during such periods!

The confession has thirty-three chapters and "all" of Christian doctrine is considered from the creation to the last judgment. The predestination of Calvin is expounded, but free will
is also covered. The covenant of works with Adam is noted, as
is the covenant of grace made in Christ. Headliners are a definition of sin (Question 14); what God is (Question 4); and the
chief end of humankind (Question 1)—all in the Shorter Catechism. The Westminster Confession was amended through
the years by Presbyterian churches in this country; the Larger
Catechism was dropped by the United Presbyterian Church in
the U.S.A. at the time of the adoption of the *Book of Confessions*
in 1967, but was reinstated in 1983 in church reunion since it
had remained in the confessional documents of the Presbyterian Church in the United States.

The Contemporary Creeds

1. The Theological Declaration of Barmen

Written in 1934, at the time Adolf Hitler was bringing every
institution in the Third Reich under his control, this declaration had political persuasion, passion, and power. In it, "[t]he
foundation of the Church was held to be in the Revelation of
God in Jesus Christ and not in any subordinate revelation in
nature or history, and her primary mission was defined as to
preach the Gospel of the free Grace of God."[11]

2. The Confession of 1967

The theme of this recent confession is reconciliation, and the
underlying biblical text is 2 Corinthians 5:16–21. Jack Rogers
writes:

The confession was presented in three parts. First was
"God's Work of Reconciliation," through Jesus Christ,

through the Love of God, and through the Communion of the Holy Spirit. The role of the Bible was treated in a subsection on the Spirit. Second was "The Ministry of Reconciliation," divided into discussions of the Mission of the Church, which included reconciliation in society, and the Equipment of the Church, which included a discussion of preaching and teaching and the sacraments. Third was "The Fulfillment of Reconciliation" in the totality of human life in its environment and in the culmination of God's kingdom.[12]

There were those who objected to beginning with anything other than the Bible, but increasingly the church accepted the appropriateness of beginning with Jesus Christ, the Word of God. The confession says, "Confessions and declarations are subordinate standards in the church, subject to the authority of Jesus Christ, the Word of God, as the Scriptures bear witness to him" (Preface, 9.03). Others found it difficult to get used to the idea of including contemporary issues in a creed. In section 4 on "Reconciliation in Society," the topics are the family; peace, justice, and freedom among nations; poverty; and sexual relationships—all quite unusual subjects in a creed. The single phrase that caused the most trouble was "even at risk to national security" in efforts "to reduce areas of strife and to broaden international understanding." Partly as the novelty wore off and increasingly as the church considered the necessity to put Christ over the nation, the church has agreed, that, as had been argued at Barmen, this was, indeed, where the church ought to stand, and be bold about it.

3. A Brief Statement of Faith

The composition of the Special Committee that first drafted A Brief Statement was quite diverse, as we have noted, to the extent that many prophesied that it would be impossible for that committee to reach agreement on anything, except, possibly, adjournment! In fact, it was not only the committee, but the entire church that accepted the document with enthusiasm

and deep appreciation. One of the features that has commended this statement has been its adaptability for use in
worship, even though it is, of course, much longer than the
frequently used Apostles' Creed. The accompanying Intro-
ductory Guide is also quite usable for study.

Presbyterians would call it providence (there is no such
thing as luck in Reformed theology) that A Brief Statement reviews the same issues that are found in chapter II of the *Book of
Order.*

The opening line, "In life and in death we belong to God,"
is reminiscent of the first question in the Heidelberg Catechism, noted earlier. Readers immediately look to what is often referred to as the Apostolic Benediction (in 2 Corinthians
13:14 [13]) when they see lines 2–4: "Through the grace of our
Lord Jesus Christ, the love of God, and the communion of the
Holy Spirit." Active church people promptly feel at home!

The trinitarian formula follows, but for traditionalists there
may be a shock to find that instead of God, Christ, and Spirit,
the order of the first two is reversed. The first section begins,
"We trust in Jesus Christ," similar to the way in which the
Confession of 1967 begins in Part I, with "The grace of our
Lord Jesus Christ." In parallel fashion, the second section is,
"We trust in God," and the third, "We trust in God the Holy
Spirit." It is trinitarian, both traditional and with a flair for the
refreshing change of pace.

The first section takes us swirling back in time to the Council of Nicaea and the Nicene Creed, "fully human, fully God"
instead of the ancient "Very God of Very God" with the concomitant stress also on the humanity of Jesus. Following close
upon the "being" of Jesus is the proclamation of the Christ:
"the reign of God, preaching good news to the poor and release to the captives . . . , healing the sick and binding up the
brokenhearted . . . ," referring us back in time to Isaiah 61:1–2;
Matthew 25; and Luke 4. The "call to repent" was the message
of both John the Baptist and Jesus. Then comes the shocker:
Jesus was "unjustly condemned for blasphemy and sedition."
How political can you get? This does not suggest Sallman's

calm and sedate artistic rendering of the *Head of Christ*, because this language is appropriate for a revolutionary.

The next section on God uses typical language at the beginning and then says, "God . . . makes everyone equally in
God's image, male and female, of every race and people, to
live as one community." Hurrah for the Presbyterian Church
(U.S.A.), vintage about A.D. 2000. Sadly, such words would not
have been used in creed or sermon often in every Presbyterian
pulpit until recent times. Mercifully, God has brought us to
this place—together! In beautiful, descriptive language, this
section expresses other venerable truths of the faith. Until,
that is, we read that we ". . . threaten death to the planet," an
expression of our own era.

Then there is the inclusive language, "the God of Abraham
and Sarah," and then in wonderful imagery, "Loving us still,
God makes us heirs with Christ of the covenant. Like a
mother who will not forsake her nursing child, like a father
who runs to welcome the prodigal home, God is faithful still."
And the vibrant joy is that the entire church shares these perceptions.

It is not some modern psychologist or social worker, but the
Presbyterian Church (U.S.A.)'s confessional statement that
says, "The Spirit . . . sets us free to accept ourselves." Other
statements about the work of the Spirit are more routine,
though expressed in contemporary words and phrases with
the subject in line 66, "the Spirit gives us courage," until line
69: "to unmask idolatries in Church and culture." If there are
places where Christians need insight as well as courage it is in
unmasking idolatries in both the church and the secular
world. Through the convictions stated in this creed, thirty
years after the Confession of 1967, the church is reminded of
this difficult but indispensable responsibility in facing cultural
twists, turns, and fads.

Then near the ending is an extremely timely summary quotation from Romans 8:38 and 39: "[W]e rejoice that nothing in
life or in death can separate us from the love of God in Christ
Jesus our Lord." A wonderful creed that unites us!

Our God, our help in ages past,
Our hope for years to come,
Our shelter from the stormy blast,
And our eternal home:

Before the hills in order stood,
Or earth received its frame,
From everlasting Thou art God,
To endless years the same.

A thousand ages in Thy sight
Are like an evening gone;
Short as the watch that ends the night
Before the rising sun.

Time, like an ever rolling stream,
Soon bears us all away;
We fly forgotten, as a dream
Dies at the opening day.

Our God, our help in ages past,
Our hope for years to come,
Be Thou our guard while life shall last,
And our eternal home.

(Isaac Watts)[13]

5

From Pole to Pole
"The Church and Its Mission"

"Mitto, mittere, misi, missus." Latin students of all ages readily recall the verb *mitto* in its various principal parts. The English word is "send," or "to send." The mission of the church is sending the good news of Jesus Christ![1] Each of us sent is a missionary, one who carries the message.

At the General Assembly of 1831 in Philadelphia, Dr. John Holt Rice stated that "the Presbyterian Church in the United States is a missionary society, . . . and every member of the Church is a member for life of said society . . . !"[2] If there is one aspect of the Presbyterian church that has characterized it through and through, it is that it is a mission-minded church. We are bound together programmatically and in financial support to this cause, probably more than to any other.

Persons who were not members of the Presbyterian Church before 1983 may not know that chapter 3 on mission is new in the *Book of Order*, and in a clarion call this chapter spells out the implications of the fundamental invitation, indeed, duty, to be about the task of mission.

We join God's activity in the world

In magnificent fashion this new chapter in the *Book of Order* identifies the mission of the church today as a continuation of God's work through history. This is very humbling for us, but very challenging, as we earnestly seek to discern and fulfill the will of God. Early paragraphs in this chapter of the *Book of Order* spell out the activity of God which we have believed and understood to be true; then the covenant of God is described. Here are the words:

> God created the heavens and the earth and made human beings in God's image, charging them to care for all that lives; God made men and women to live in community, responding to their Creator with grateful obedience. Even when the human race broke community with its Maker and with one another, God did not forsake it, but out of grace chose one family for the sake of all, to be pilgrims of promise, God's own Israel.
>
> God liberated the people of Israel from oppression; God covenanted with Israel to be their God and they to be God's people, that they might do justice, love mercy, and walk humbly with the Lord; God confronted Israel with the responsibilities of this covenant, judging people for their unfaithfulness while sustaining them by divine grace. (G-3.0101a–b)

And this is our rule book! The mission of the church is none other than to continue God's work in the world. If we have ever searched the scriptures diligently, probed the lessons from antiquity, and carefully developed a social analysis about our culture and clime with the avowed purpose of deciding what God's word is for today, now is that time. Where and how is God leading us? Our need is to immerse ourselves in the Bible and both parts of our Constitution: the *Book of Confessions*, and somewhat surprisingly, our *Book of Order*.

It is always an especially thrilling time at a baptism when the minister names the child or adult being baptized, and immediately following the name, says, *child of the covenant*." One part of the mission of the church is being performed when a child of believers, or when a believer, is being identified with the whole history of God's covenant people. The mission of that church is to be God's agent in calling people to be faithful followers of Jesus Christ.

It is truly remarkable, then, that despite our differences in what we discerned, or thought we understood, in God's activity that we have agreed so fundamentally about our mission past, present, and future. Our styles of proceeding in the continuation of God's activities in the world will always diverge according to our varying perceptions; nevertheless, we maintain a significant unity in working together on those tasks that we all understand to be the proper and appropriate mission of the church.

We all agree (as does our Constitution) that we have received the gospel (been elected by God) not to keep it ourselves, but to share it with all the world. Presbyterians are united in believing that the church exists to make a difference in the world. This is what truly unites Presbyterians.

Mission is what is constitutive of the church

This is the church as the Body of Christians indicated in the *Book of Order* chapter on "The Church and Its Mission." The marching orders of the church to an earlier generation of Presbyterians are Jesus' final words to his disciples in the Gospel of Matthew, often referred to as the Great Commission:

When they saw him, they worshiped him; but some doubted. And Jesus came and said to them, "All authority in heaven and on earth has been given to me. Go therefore and make disciples of all nations, baptizing them in the name of the Father and of the Son and of the Holy Spirit, and teaching them to obey everything that I have commanded you. And remember, I am with you always, to the end of the age." (Matt. 28:17–20)

Eugene Peterson has a fascinating rendering of this passage:

The moment they saw him they worshipped him. Some, though, held back, not sure about risking themselves totally.

Jesus, undeterred, went right ahead and gave his charge: "God authorized and commanded me to commission you: Go out and train everyone you meet, far and near, in this way of life, marking them by baptism in the threefold name: Father, Son, and Holy Spirit. Then instruct them in the practice of all I have commanded you. I'll be with you as you do this, day after day after day, right up to the end of the age."[3]

These familiar words of Jesus given to his disciples echo throughout this chapter. There was a time in the Presbyterian Church, and in other denominations similar to ours, where what has sometimes been called "the salt water syndrome" existed. That is, mission was perceived to be something that the church in the United States engaged in through its supporting financially and sending across the ocean—the salt water— salaried missionaries. Since we the authors have been engaged in that enterprise for many years, we do not take it lightly or dismiss it in any way.

There seems to be a much better balance today, however, in the emphasis on church members being "missionaries" right where they live in this country, that is, having a missionary intention about their occupations and their recreation, all dedicated to the glory of God. This kind of local mission is not nearly so glamorous in the minds of most people, but there is a certain integrity about it as "ordinary" Christians are practicing their witness and service in areas where they live instead of placing undue stress on paying professionals to do their mission work for them elsewhere. In the language of this chapter they are demonstrating that "the Church of Jesus Christ is the provisional demonstration of what God intends for all humanity."

A combination of informed and intelligent comprehension of Isaiah 61; the messages of Amos, Micah, and Hosea; Matthew 25; and Luke 4 resonates with the description in the chapter on mission (see G-3.0300c(3)). This portion of the chapter in the *Book of Order* gives a much broader scope and vision of mission than limiting the work of the church to just Matthew 28, as far-reaching as that passage is.

What these extensive words mean to us is certainly that the work of the particular church and of each governing body is not just the bare bones kind of thing that we often regard as "our job" as active Presbyterians. One reason for our limited thinking of our duties and responsibilities can be traced to the questions asked when session minutes are examined. Did each meeting of the session open and close with prayer? Yes. Were the minutes of the previous meeting read and approved? Yes. Do the records indicate that the session voted to serve communion, and is the later notation there that communion was duly served? Yes. Were the newly elected church officers examined before they were ordained and/or installed? Yes. Was the report given from the last meeting of presbytery? Yes. Was the treasurer's report discussed in sufficient detail for everyone to have been satisfied? Oh, my, yes. Then, Did we "engage in the struggle to free people from sin, fear, oppression, hunger, and injustice?" Did we do what!? You've got to be kidding.

Another way that this section makes sense to some of us is to think of having a *moral audit* of the minutes, that is to say, how, what, when, and where is the session—and its congregation—fulfilling its responsibility to be about the mission of Christ in this place, in the vicinity of our particular church, across our vast land, and around the world. Our processes and procedures are important as all clerks of session and governing body stated clerks can verify, but it is vital for the session and other governing bodies to review periodically what that body has done, is doing, and is planning to do in light of these broad mission duties and responsibilities. Getting bogged down in the routine seems so easy, while viewing the task of the church from a broad perspective is demanding, challenging, and frequently more work than had been anticipated.

Jesus said, "Those who find their life will lose it, and those who lose their life for my sake will find it" (Matt. 10:39)

The similar language in the *Book of Order* is, "The Church is called to undertake this mission even at the risk of losing its life, trusting in God alone as the author and giver of life, sharing the gospel, and doing those deeds in the world that point beyond themselves to the new reality in Christ" (G-3.0400). The Presbyterian Church is not divided in facing a clear temptation. Most of us are quite comfortable, thank you, with our belief in Christ as Redeemer, and without being judgmental, we recognize that most of us are content to be in the respectable Presbyterian Church. The evil reality often is that we are too comfortable, we wish to stay the way we are, and here is the joker: We desire to keep our religion—for us. Too few of us have the zeal and passion to share our faith, or "to lose our lives" for the sake of Christ and the gospel. The call of Christ is just the opposite. A church in mission is a giving church—of itself, of its resources, of its leadership, its joys and its pleasures, and, yes, of its perquisites, which sometimes means status.

In the minds of many Presbyterians this is radical talk. "Radical" here does not mean basic and fundamental as it did in 1797, as used in the first chapter in the *Book of Order*, but radical in the sense of a marked departure from the usually accepted norm of what most people expect to be the case. The portion of the chapter under consideration goes on, "The Church is called . . . to a new openness to its own membership, by affirming itself as a community of diversity, becoming in fact as well as in faith a community of women and men of all ages, races, and conditions, and by providing for inclusiveness as a visible sign of the new humanity" (G-3.0401b).

This is a book about what unites Presbyterians. We must be careful and accurate in saying that this final point on this chapter is, in fact, where the Presbyterian Church (U.S.A.) stands united. Certainly, it can be stated that in accepting and approving this *Book of Order* the representatives of our church did stand united and agree that this language and the thoughts behind the words are a fair and acceptable understanding of where this church is—or at least wants to be. It is appropriate, in any case, for continuing discussions to take place in the church about precisely what the ongoing mission of this denomination is and should be. And, of course, each session, each presbytery, and each synod should be encouraged to have its own continuing struggle to define and redefine its understanding of its mission.

Or what about the statement, in this same section, that "[t]he Church is called . . . to a more joyous celebration in worship and work"?

Concentrating on a joyful joining in mission can stir a session, presbytery, synod, or General Assembly! Lonely isolation can be a debilitating illness of the body, and of the spirit. A novel approach to discerning what God might be calling us to be and do in mission might be more rewarding if we deliberately try to squash any isolation we may feel by physically meeting with others. One proven way of enlarging a vision or of conceiving of different ways of tackling an assignment is when elders from several congregations—if they are not too far physically removed from others—periodically have a retreat together to share what each is doing and what might be better done together, regardless of slight philosophical or theological differences, to say nothing about working together across racial or ethnic lines or economic/class divisions. No one session needs *always* to meet just by itself, and the larger configuration does not always have to be a presbytery or some similar gathering, such as an area cluster of the local council of churches.

Strangely, our being united virtually forces us to attest that we normally do just the routine mundane ecclesiastical tasks. We can be bound together in facing the larger and far more complex, or provocative, or even controversial jobs for which we might be labeled seditious, or, at the least, extremely radical or nontraditional. If any session is timid about embarking on strange waters, strength can be found in joining other sessions (or just one other) in testing how they feel the wind of the Spirit might be blowing. Then consideration can come about weighing anchor from "the way things have always been done here" to steer the ecclesiastical ship across uncharted seas in mission and outreach. It may not be immediately transparent that this chapter is more demanding and suggestive than we ordinarily comprehend the work of the Presbyterian Church to be, but has the time not arrived for hard questions about faithfulness to be posed, and should that summons not include a more careful reading and study of our common calling as illustrated and described in this chapter? You see, the language here is quite descriptive and inclusive:

> The church is called to present the claims of Jesus Christ, leading persons to repentance, acceptance of him as Savior and Lord, and new life as his disciples . . . , participating in God's activity in the world through its life for others by
>
> (a) healing and reconciling and binding up wounds,
> (b) ministering to the needs of the poor, the sick, the lonely, and the powerless,
> (c) engaging in the struggle to free people from sin, fear, oppression, hunger, and injustice,
> (d) giving itself and its substance to the service of those who suffer,
> (e) sharing with Christ in the establishing of his just, peaceable, and loving rule in the world.
>
> (G-3.0300b–c(3))

Perhaps even more pertinent is this. Would we have time, money and emotional energy to be finding fault with each other's orthodoxy and the way we do things if we were to devote ourselves with renewed energy to an entirely new and challenging way of conceiving ministry in Christ's name?

Yes, the church (with all its members) is committed (1) to join God's activity in the world; (2) to recognize that mission is what constitutes the church in a major way; and, most remarkable of all, (3) to undertake mission *even at the risk of losing its life*.

> Blest be the tie that binds
> Our hearts in Christian love:
> The fellowship of kindred minds
> Is like to that above.

Before our Father's* throne
We pour our ardent prayers;
Our fears, our hopes, our aims are one,
Our comforts and our cares.

We share our mutual woes,
Our mutual burdens bear,
And often for each other flows
The sympathizing tear.

From sorrow, toil, and pain,
And sin we shall be free;
And perfect love and friendship reign
Through all eternity.

(John Fawcett)[4]

---

* Or "Maker's"

6

"All for One and One for All"

"The Church and Its Unity"
in the *Book of Order*

A missionary of our denomination was seeking one day to explain to a visitor some personal observations and convictions about the citizens of the country where the missionary served. The illustration was this: "The people of this country are terrible volleyball players, but they are excellent at ping pong." The point was: these dear folks are superb at one-on-one kinds of things, but they do not cooperate very well with each other. A pertinent question for the Presbyterian Church (U.S.A.) in a similar framework is: Do we do well at ping pong, or volleyball, or both?

It is our contention that the fourth chapter in the *Book of Order*[1] suggests three affirmative statements, and this chapter is divided into these three emphases: (1) The Presbyterian Church (U.S.A.) is committed to unity in Christ's church; (2) the Presbyterian Church (U.S.A.) is committed to unity within the Presbyterian Church; (3) the Presbyterian Church (U.S.A.) is committed to unity, but not by being all alike. Diversity is appropriate and important.

The Presbyterian Church (U.S.A.)
is committed to unity in Christ's church

In the *Presbyterian Survey* of September 1987, Robert McAfee Brown wrote, "I am a Presbyterian—therefore I am ecumenical. . . . To be ecumenical is as Presbyterian as predestination. . . . [It] never was the intention of John Calvin, John Knox or other Presbyterian forebears to 'divide' the church." They "conceived of themselves as doing just the opposite—recovering the heritage of the early *un*divided church."[2] The confessions have the happy facility of enabling us readily and easily to realize that we are not alone, but that we stand with that great company worldwide which celebrates and testifies with the apostle Paul, "There is one body and one Spirit, just as you were called to the one hope of your calling, one Lord, one faith, one baptism, one God and Father of all, who is above all and through all and in all" (Eph. 4:4–6).

The *Book of Order* reference in chapter IV is: "The Church universal consists of all persons in every nation, together with their children, who profess faith in Jesus Christ as Lord and Savior and commit themselves to live in a fellowship under his rule" (G-4.0101). And further, "Since this whole company cannot meet together in one place to worship and to serve, it is reasonable that it should be divided into particular congregations. The particular church is, therefore, understood as a local expression of the universal Church" (G-4.0102).

It is absolutely essential that Presbyterians continue to understand that the Presbyterian Church (U.S.A.) is not *the* church, but *a part of* the church. With the apostle Paul we have affirmed again and again that we are a part of one body, and that with Brown we understand that we are constantly seeking to recover our heritage as an integral part of the undivided church. This is the heart and soul of our understanding of the church of Jesus Christ. Given that presupposition, we can catch the ecumenical vision of knowing, loving, and being related to our brothers and sisters in other "parts" of the church universal.

One only has to worship in a packed church in Shanghai, China, in the balcony with a cluster of other foreigners from different lands to feel a lump in the throat as the congregation sings energetically in Chinese the second stanza of "The Church's One Foundation," and to remember the words in English, "Elect from every nation, yet one o'er all the earth,"[3] to feel and *know* that you are a part of something much bigger than you may have often thought. The Form of Government reminds us that the confessions reenforce our understanding that we belong to the one, holy, catholic, and apostolic church.

We read in chapter IV in the *Book of Order*: "The unity of the Church is a gift of its Lord and finds expression in its faithfulness to the mission to which Christ calls it. The Church is a fellowship of believers which seeks the enlargement of the circle of faith to include all people and is never content to enjoy the benefits of Christian community for itself alone" (G-4.0201).

This is the clear theological underpinning for the strong, consistent, and historical mission policy overseas of our church to work with and support and assist, as we are able, our partner churches in each country where we work. It is our conviction that in God's economy the national church of a country is the instrument God uses to continue God's activities in evangelism, nurture, and service in that land. Mission and unity walk hand in hand.[4]

With a historic commitment to Christian unity, it is no wonder that Presbyterians helped establish and were charter members of: (1) the World Alliance of Reformed Churches (the 1970 union of the 1875 World Presbyterian Alliance and the 1891 International Congregational Council); (2) the Federal Council of Churches in 1908; and its successor, (3) the National Council of the Churches of Christ in the U.S.A. (NCC) in 1950; and (4) the World Council of Churches, organized in 1948. From their founding the Federal, then National, and the World Councils have had exemplary leadership from Presbyterians. Presbyterian Samuel McCrea Cavert was long the executive of the Federal Council, and then the National Council. One of his successors was Presbyterian Claire Randall, and recent presidents of the NCC were Presbyterians Syngman Rhee and Patricia McClurg. Presbyterian Eugene Carson Blake was the second General Secretary of the World Council. Presbyterians have held many elected positions and many staff positions in these various ecumenical organizations. As Robert McAfee Brown indicated, such participation is of the essence of being Presbyterian—it is the Presbyterian ethos.

Not every Presbyterian has had the privilege and the thrill of witnessing the accomplishments in mission which in many instances could not have happened had there not been full ecumenical cooperation. One of many similar illustrations could be told over again about other such occurrences. A devastating earthquake shook many villages several years ago in a particular section of the Middle East, causing great destruction and loss of life. The Anglican and Evangelical Presbyterian churches wished to share in the relief response, but even their pooled funds would be insufficient to do much, and, besides, they lacked expertise in responding to such an emergency. Quickly, a request for assistance went to the offices of the World Council of Churches (WCC) in Geneva.

The World Council responded promptly and WCC representatives met with local representatives, including those from the Roman Catholic, Armenian Orthodox, and other churches, to discuss what might be done. When the decision was made to cooperate with the government and other agencies, it was agreed that the Christians would completely rebuild one small village. The World Council experts in funding, construction, and other fields, in cooperation with national Christians, did a wonderful job of working with the villagers in the master rebuilding plan. The Christian community involvement could never have meant much without everyone's working under the auspices of the World Council.

This kind of cooperative aid to human suffering has become almost routine around the world. In conflict situations, such as those beginning in the mid-1990s in Africa, World Council teams have both provided emergency relief and also sought to be a part of the process of providing resolution among the warring bodies, some of which have been Christian.

An entirely different kind of ecumenical cooperation in which Presbyterians have been heavily involved has been the writing, publishing, distribution, and use of the annual superb mission study books of Friendship Press. Presbyterian representatives help decide the ecumenical mission themes for a number of years ahead and suggest possible authors of the books for adults and the various age groups, what kinds of materials would be particularly appropriate, and so on. There are surely very few Presbyterians who have never benefited from one or more of these excellent study materials on mission—a theme annually for a nation, region, or religion overseas, as well as a subject for study and possible help in those groups most in need in the United States.

A recent example of outstanding National Council of Churches of Christ leadership in mission and pastoral care has been in calling member communions to participate vigorously in assisting the members and leaders of those predominantly African American churches which have been burned, presumably motivated by racist attitudes.

State and area councils of churches, in addition to (sometimes) metropolitan councils of churches, virtually always prominently including Presbyterians, have planned and executed an abundance of mission projects for state, area, or city. Recruiting and supporting chaplains in all kinds of penal, mental health, retirement, or state medical institutions have become so common as to be almost invisible. Similarly, these same coalitions have come together for purposes ranging from studying how best the community can responsibly deal with drug addiction to how best to plan new church development in new housing areas to avoid unneeded competition between and among denominations so one religious group can plant a new church in one area, while upon agreement another denomination would sponsor a new church development in an area some distance away.

Retreats, camping programs, campus ministries, Church Women United, Christian services in national or state parks during the summer, and the like, have been either tangentially related or completely sponsored by a local, regional, or national council of churches. To be sure, many of these mission efforts have been headed by Presbyterian elders, members, or ministers. Almost anyone could add to the list of ecumenical mission programs or projects.

It may seem odd that there can be two kinds of calls for ecumenical cooperation in mission, and that those kinds of ecumenical groupings remain separate from each other. More conservative Christians have felt that their more liberal sisters and brothers in the faith placed too much emphasis in their unity on social justice kinds of issues, and that they did not give sufficient attention to evangelism. Thus, when the Billy Graham organization sponsored an International Congress of World Evangelization in Lausanne, Switzerland, in 1974, neither the PCUS nor the UPCUSA participated officially in this event, but many individual Presbyterians did attend. Ever since, the one word, "Lausanne," has identified the cause that brought that group into being. There are still definite distinctions between the World Council of Churches and the Lausanne group, but in the intervening years the issued statements and concerns have sounded increasingly similar.

The meetings of the "official" denomination-related and World Council of Churches–related Conferences on World Mission and Evangelism have continued. The Presbyterian Church (U.S.A.) continues to work with and through partner churches around the world, and not just through its Worldwide Ministries Division as a missionary sending agency. The operating principles in global mission of our denomination are explored in chapter 10 of this book.

Through both formal and informal groups Presbyterians have worked with others in student work on campuses, notably through the World Student Christian Federation (with Presbyterian Francis Pickens Miller at the helm for a number of years) and United Ministries in Higher Education; many Presbyterians have been involved with groups such as Campus Crusade and the triennial Urbana Mission Conference. In mass media Presbyterians have worked with various state councils of churches, as well as with the National Council of Churches. Many present-day Christian groups such as Habitat for Humanity have the committed participation and support of many Presbyterians and their congregations.

The authors of *The Re-Forming Tradition* assert, "As organizational ecumenism has withered, popular ecumenism has triumphed. Its acceptance of religious diversity, due sometimes to theological indifference, is a striking feature of late-twentieth-century America."[5]

New forms of Christian unity are being called for in various quarters. In November 1996, the Central Committee of the World Council of Churches sent a Vision Statement to member churches of the World Council of Churches.[6] This draft document for possible restructuring of the World Council included these words: "Special attention should be given to enabling participation by the Roman Catholic Church and by evangelical and Pentecostal bodies who are partners in one ecumenical movement."[7] The World Council might be just one body in such a new configuration. S. Mark Heim has written, "The rationale of the modern ecumenical movement still holds: there is a scriptural and intrinsic mandate for unity. This traditional rationale itself calls for a new and broadened movement. The credibility of our desire for unity hinges on the proportion of the Christian community we are willing to engage."[8]

There are many informal ways in which Presbyterians unite with other Christians. As all Presbyterians appreciate, we "read each other's theologies," biblical commentaries, and missiological studies. Father Raymond Brown is not only a seminal Roman Catholic writer on biblical material, but he is also a prolific and a very thorough writer. His commentaries on the Gospel of John in the Anchor Bible series, for instance, are "must" reading for the expositor. Doing theology today without reference to Roman Catholic Hans Küng would be like driving a car with only three tires full of air. It has been quite natural, in the past several years, to have a noted Roman Catholic priest-author teach about culture sensitivity issues at missionary orientation conferences for Presbyterians and Evangelical Lutherans, meeting jointly. The conferees routinely visit, talk with, and learn from places and people in various kinds of non-Presbyterian and Presbyterian mission in the host city of such a conference.

When discussing ecumenicity, one major section of the Presbyterian Church (U.S.A.) clearly means church-to-church relationships. Further, these relationships are official ones that come into being by action of governing bodies or through one of the boards or agencies of the church.

"Ecumenical" has meant the working together of official church bodies, with much less thought now than was true some years ago of their having organic union. The newer "ecumenical groups" in the church understand ecumenical to be something quite different, at least for part of the time. These ties are also across denominational or national lines, but they are not official groupings; rather they are a coming together in organizations or groups of people who have chosen to work for a particular cause, or to share common approaches in mission. Not necessarily working through an official governing body, these groups are designated usually by the term "parachurch" groups or organizations. Tensions sometimes arise between these two meanings and understandings of being ecumenical. One group is related to and reporting to a church governing body; the other group often raises money and performs work that is felt to be just as important, and it is developed in a manner that the governing bodies of the church cannot or will not undertake.

Parachurch groups have been around for a long time. The earliest overseas mission work by Presbyterians was done through the American Board of Commissioners for Foreign Missions, really a joint mission effort by Congregationalists and Presbyterians before the Presbyterian General Assembly established a Presbyterian Board of Foreign Missions in 1837. Through the years all three of the former denominations now united in our church had women's missionary outreach of one kind or another, and they were parachurch organizations before being taken under the denominational umbrella. The YMCA and YWCA, the American Bible Society of an earlier time, and Habitat for Humanity today are illustrations of one kind of parachurch mission thrust, while World Vision, Inter-Varsity, and various faith missions are illustrative of parachurch organizations hard at work today.

Reports and actions from such denominationally oriented

ecumenical organizations as the World Council of Churches today sound much like reports and actions from various program-oriented ecumenical groups such as the Lausanne Conference. The denominationally oriented ecumenical groups were once much more supportive of human rights and social witness causes, but now some of the groups often called evangelical are heavily involved even in direct political action.

The Presbyterian Church (U.S.A.) is committed to unity within the Presbyterian Church

Over the last thirty years we have seen not only two major Presbyterian reunions (which we celebrate), but also painful church divisions: the departure of those who formed the Presbyterian Church in America and the Evangelical Presbyterian Church. Further, not only have congregations formally withdrawn, but also many others have withdrawn emotionally, withholding funds and minimizing their connections with the broader body of the Presbyterian Church (U.S.A.). Also, over the last thirty years a profusion of interest groups have developed within the Presbyterian Church (U.S.A.), often at odds with one another and the governing bodies. We have had major conflicts over the church's social witness, re-imagining, and the role of gay and lesbian Christians in the church. Trust, respect, and civility have often been the casualties of these conflicts.

The chapter on unity in the *Book of Order* has some salient sentences, such as this: "The Presbyterian system of government calls for continuity with and faithfulness to the heritage which lies behind the contemporary church. It calls equally for openness and faithfulness to the renewing activity of the God of history" (G-4.0303). We did not arrive here on our own. We are just the present actors on the stage of the drama of God at work in the world, our world, and we will not even receive Oscar nominations by the quality of our great performances, but by the grace and mercy that God has shed and does shed on God's people. Nevertheless, the response to God's faithfulness is our thanksgiving and praise for the kind of God we know, and to show forth the same qualities of covenant love that God has showered upon us creatures.

First Corinthians 12 contains a profound treatment of unity in diversity:

> For just as the body is one and has many members, and all the members of the body, though many, are one body, so it is with Christ. For in the one Spirit we were all baptized into one body—Jews or Greeks, slaves or free—and we were all made to drink of one Spirit.
> Indeed, the body does not consist of one member but of many. If the foot would say, "Because I am not a hand, I do not belong to the body," that would not make it any less a part of the body. And if the ear would say, "Because I am not an eye, I do not belong to the body," that would not make it any less a part of the body. If the whole body were an eye, where would hearing be? If the whole body were hearing, where would the sense of smell be? But as it is, God arranged the members in the body, each one of them, as he chose. If all were a single member, where would the body be? As it is, there are many members, yet one body. The eye cannot say to the hand, "I have no need of you," nor again the head to the feet, "I have no need of you." On the contrary, the members of the body that seem to be weaker are indispensable, and those members that we think less honorable we clothe with greater honor. . . .
> Now you are the body of Christ and individually members of it. . . . apostles, . . . prophets, . . . teachers; . . . Are all apostles? Are all prophets? Are all teachers?
> (1 Cor. 12:12–23, 27–29)

Quite obviously, each of us is different, and each has a reserved seat in the stadium of life, and a function. We are not all Buckeyes from Ohio, nor Tarheels from North Carolina, nor Sooners from Oklahoma, nor Thais from Thailand, nor Senegalese, nor Eskimos, nor Brazilians, nor women, nor are we all left-handed, nor blond, nor short; but God makes it clear to us that we all belong. The problem comes when we want to exclude, to discriminate, and to read some out of the club.

Regardless of our differences we are united in the body of Christ known as the Presbyterian Church (U.S.A.).

It is no accident that this chapter on the church and its unity contains the "Principles of Presbyterian Government." Unity certainly has never meant complete agreement on every subject by all participants in whatever governing body or discussion group. What it *does* mean is that, even though a person is in the minority on any specific issue, that person—and all others—understand and accept the fact that the majority opinion or conviction shall prevail. Presbyterian procedural rules provide for equal opportunity for proponents of a subject to have a fair presentation of their position, but unity is not based on whether or not any one person or that person's presentation will sway the majority. Unity is thus found in diversity, in diverse opinions and feelings about how to proceed or what the objectives may be, but always with the abiding agreement that those proposals with the majority vote shall be adopted and implemented, or lost, as the case may be.

Presbyterian polity is an instrument for unity within the church. The unity within the church is in the established procedures, to which all have agreed in advance to accept. There should be no surprises about process. The agreements on procedures include fair play in every way, meaning that each position is to be presented in complete integrity, and that also means that there will be no distortions of any position not one's own. Objectivity is extremely difficult for partisans, but unless strict honesty is held to by all, achieving—or maintaining—unity is far from certain. As members of a society that is having great trouble in meeting high standards of professional conduct, one of the places where Presbyterians can "exhibit social righteousness" is in the way we treat each and conduct our business. Scrupulous integrity is a character trait most admired by all concerned, and to whatever extent we in the church desire unity, we must abide by the highest standards, not just in our aims and purposes, but also by the way we seek to achieve results.

The Presbyterian Church (U.S.A.) must
be committed to unity, but not by being all alike

The final section in chapter IV of the *Book of Order* is both a definition of diversity and of inclusiveness and an exhortation for the church to be sensitive to persons of all kinds in myriad ways, including through having a variety of worship practices. It reads, in part:

> The church in its witness to the uniqueness of the Christian faith is called to mission and must be responsive to diversity in both the church and the world. Thus the fellowship . . . will display a rich variety of form, practice, language, program, nurture, and service to suit culture and need. (G-4.0401–2)

One of the hardest slogans to break is the familiar "We never did it that way before," often expressed with some vehemence! Probably the least welcome place for many of us to change is in the contents and order of our worship services. A test for our spoken willingness to be inclusive can be right here. Are we willing to alter our routine in worship, even by the rhythm, tempo, and volume of our music in worship, in order to accommodate or attract potential newcomers to our church? Missed chances for contacts with "strangers" can only sometimes be repeated.

It does not matter greatly what year the annual statistics are from, since they differ only slightly from year to year, but the trends are quite clear. In the United States the percentage of white Anglo-Saxons is declining, and the percentage of African Americans, Hispanics, and Asian Americans continues to climb. The 208th General Assembly (1996) action was clear: ". . . directs the General Assembly Council to provide unrestricted funds for new church development and redevelopment beginning in 1998."[9] Why? The recommended resolution from the National Ministries Division had included the following:

> Whereas, the current reality that racial ethnic membership in this denomination is only 4.7 percent when racial

ethnics are more than 20 percent of the population of the United States is a testimony of the lack of emphasis the denomination has placed in racial ethnic evangelism in spite of its current language and policies of inclusion on paper; and . . . affirms the goal of increasing the racial ethnic membership to 10 percent of the Presbyterian Church (U.S.A.) membership by the year 2005, and to 20 percent by the year 2010.[10]

As a church we are united in a determination to transform "language and policies of inclusion on paper" into reality, a task that requires not just an eye here and there, and a big toe somewhere else, but the entire body of Christ working with conviction in harmony! The beginning or starting place is normally with the proper determination of the session, which then must garner the full support of the entire congregation. We are united as a denomination, in principle, to inclusiveness, but the particular implementation often wanes.

> Called as partners in Christ's service,
> Called to ministries of grace,
> We respond with deep commitment
> Fresh new lines of faith to trace.
> May we learn the art of sharing,
> Side by side and friend with friend,
> Equal parts in our caring
> To fulfill God's chosen end.
>
> Christ's example, Christ's inspiring,
> Christ's clear call to work and worth,
> Let us follow, never faltering,
> Reconciling folk on earth.
> Men and women, richer, poorer,
> All God's people, young and old,
> Blending human skills together
> Gracious gifts from God unfold.
>
> Thus new patterns for Christ's mission,
> In a small or global sense,

Help us bear each other's burdens,
Breaking down each wall or fence.
Words of comfort, words of vision,
Words of challenge, said with care,
Bring new power and strength for action,
Make us colleagues, free and fair.

So God grant us for tomorrow
Ways to order human life
That surround each person's sorrow
With a calm that conquers strife.
Make us partners in our living,
Our compassion to increase,
Messengers of faith, thus giving
Hope and confidence and peace.

                    (Jane Parker Huber)[11]

7

It's in the Good Book
The Centrality of the Scriptures

Do you remember the first time someone suggested that your group do some brainstorming? The leader may have suggested that all present throw out ideas on the subject at hand. After about the third comment, a participant probably said, "Well, that won't work because. . . ." The leader doubtless interrupted to explain that in brainstorming you do not critique what others have expressed, although anyone may build positively on what someone else has said. Most Presbyterian leaders are broadly experienced, as illustrated below, at careful examination to be certain that things are completely all right. We know how to critique. Some of us are less experienced at scrutinizing for the purpose of affirmation, but our agreements about scripture are truly profound, and those points of congruence need explication and confirmation.

Members of most pastor nominating committees ordinarily listen to tapes of potential candidates whom they may be considering for their church. Later in the process the committee frequently will seek to listen to the person preach live, as we say these days. Presbyterian seminary students learn about preaching in many ways, and one important series of lessons is taught through having a faculty member who teaches preaching critique the budding pulpiteer. Some family dinner tables after the Sunday church service have "roast preacher." Thinking the role of the presbyter in the Reformed Church in East Berlin was related to the "presbytery," a visiting American group asked a presbyter what his role was. The somewhat surprising response from what we would call the "elder" was,

"To be sure the preacher is preaching the Bible!" It is not surprising that ministers and church members are willing and able to critique others, including preachers, and ordinarily that is appropriate.

In the life of the church there are other occasions, however, when we do more harm than good by unduly finding fault with each other when we could be seeking to discern those things about others that we support and appreciate. There is, for instance, a fundamental agreement among Presbyterians about the Bible that we sometimes fail to recognize. One tremendous illustration of our homogeneous nature is in our common rejoicing in and accepting of the identical ordination vow for ministers, elders, and deacons, found in the *Book of Order:* "Do you accept the Scriptures of the Old and New Testaments to be, by the Holy Spirit, the unique and authoritative witness to Jesus Christ in the Church universal, and God's Word to you?"[1]

Without exegeting this vow in detail, it is symbolic that all of those ordained in the Presbyterian Church (U.S.A.) have concurred in stating an acceptance—along with the over 450-year heritage of the Reformed church—that the scriptures are what we call the Old and New Testaments. This is an affirmative statement, but it is also a clear exclusion of the Apocrypha, those books which Roman Catholics accept also as being scriptural.

The Confession of 1967 has superb language about the Bible, which speaks to us most helpfully: "The one sufficient revelation of God is Jesus Christ, the Word of God incarnate, to whom the Holy Spirit bears unique and authoritative witness through the Holy Scriptures, which are received and obeyed as the word of God written. The Scriptures are not a witness among others, but the witness without parallel."[2]

When we say "by the Holy Spirit," we are saying two important but somewhat different things, and our church agrees with each. One is that the Spirit of God was in the writing of the Bible, working through those persons who wrote what we have, and nearly all of us would add, through those who edited the scriptures, as well. The other tacit belief of ours is that the Holy Spirit also enables the reader to discern what God is saying to us through the scriptures. Of course, it needs to be noted that we are not able, unaided, to comprehend everything, since it is not all perfectly clear to us, even when we use the best tools available to exegete the text.

"Unique and authoritative" is the same language in both the Confession of 1967 and in this ordination vow. The statement is clear and easy to grasp. In the idiom of today: It says it all. That phrase does not just hang out there, of course, for it acts as a modifier of "witness to Jesus Christ in the Church universal." Others may tell us about what God in Christ has done for them, and that can be a powerful testimony, but it is scripture, not what others say, which is the unique and authoritative witness to Christ.

We will now turn to an apparently largely unknown and seldom used document on the Bible, *Biblical Authority and Interpretation*,[3] received by the 194th General Assembly (1982) of the United Presbyterian Church in the U.S.A.

We will begin by reviewing the suggested offered "guidelines" at the end of this report to the General Assembly. It seems to us that there are five points here which are very helpful, indeed, and around which we can unanimously rally. The report calls these "basic rules for the interpretation of Scripture that are summarized from the Book of Confessions." One might conclude that there is a summary somewhere of rules for interpretation found in the confessions. That is not the case. The committee prepared this list, which seemed to the committee to summarize what the confessions say on this subject.

Recognize that Jesus Christ, the Redeemer, is the center of Scripture. The redemptive activity of God is central to the entire Scripture. The Old Testament themes of the covenant and the messiah testify to this activity. In the center of the New Testament is Jesus Christ: the Word made flesh, the fulfillment of Israel's messianic hope, and the promise of the Kingdom. It is to Christ that the church witnesses. When interpreting Scripture, keeping Christ in the center aids in evaluating the significance of the problems and controversies that always persist in the vigorous, historical life of the church.[4]

Few candidates, if any, being examined before a presbytery would use this exact language, but virtually all, we believe, would subscribe to the substance of the vital importance of placing Jesus Christ at the heart of the interpretation of the Bible. In a chapter called "The Drama of Redemption," Randolph Crump Miller used five words, or themes, for giving a broad outline for the Bible, and, of course, Christ was at the center: "Creation, Covenant, Christ, Church, and Consummation."[5]

There is no question whatsoever but that the Presbyterian Church (U.S.A.), by any poll or vote, would be unanimous in agreeing about the core of our faith.

Let the focus be on the plain text of Scripture, to the grammatical and historical context, rather than to allegory or subjective fantasy.[6]

The allegorical interpretation of scripture is not currently in fashion, so this phrase may not mean so much today, but in eras when people are likely to consider all biblical material as just allegorical in nature, this statement is necessary. *Of course* we interpret the Bible in its historical context, we say, but the reality is that some devout Christians care little about what scholars agree was the time in which a specified passage was probably written. Further, typical church members do not know Hebrew and Greek (and not all ministers are fully comfortable with the biblical languages), so most of them have to take someone else's word for what the grammar was in the original text.

A somewhat far-fetched illustration may not be so far from the mark, after all. About seventy-five years ago, a Presbyterian minister was conducting a series of revival meetings in the Kentucky mountains, and he was staying in the home of devout church members. At morning worship in the home one day the guest read about Saul in the book of Acts. Afterward a family member asked him why Saul with all of his power and status in Israel was standing as a witness to the stoning of Stephen. It became apparent that the family had never realized that *King Saul* in the Old Testament was someone different from *Saul of Tarsus* who became the apostle Paul. The historical context had never previously been explained to them.

There will always be debate about some passages, especially about the period in which they were written, and, therefore, about whom they were originally intended for. Disagreement about conclusions does not invalidate, in any way, the conviction that every effort must be made by the readers of scripture to search for as much information and understanding as possible about entire biblical books, as well as about individual chapters and verses. As imperfect creatures, even the most scholarly and pious can never hope to be absolutely certain about each and every aspect of the vast material contained in the Old and New Testaments.

"Depend upon the guidance of the Holy Spirit in interpreting and applying God's message."[7] Given human fallibility, we are virtually obliged to state in a strong, affirmative manner that, without doubt, we rely on God's Spirit to direct us in the proper direction as we are guided in both the understanding and the application of scripture. In passing, we should mention that we are fortunate in each passing year that we have more insight into what Christians have discovered about biblical texts, the use of language in a given area geographically and chronologically, and the history of ancient civilizations, because of the continuing discoveries by archaeologists and through the insights and perceptions of scholars as they have pored over the biblical material. In all of history, there has never been a time like our own, when literally reams of manuscripts, books and scholarly commentaries, atlases, and extensive research have been enticingly displayed for pastors and people. We could be the most prepared people in history to comment intelligently and meaningfully on scripture both in detail and from the broad perspective. We are, indeed, blessed. And, mercifully, we are in deep concurrence about the need to apply that which we agree is before us to use. The General Assembly committee that made this report on biblical interpretation also understood our situation well, when it made the report's next point: **"[Let us] Be guided by the doctrinal consensus of the church, which is the rule of faith."**[8] There is, of course, no complete "consensus" today, but the primary consensus is far greater than we often realize or accept. In a ringing chorus we unite in accepting the centrality of scripture, and of Jesus Christ as the focal point of that scripture. Further, we with "one heart and voice" turn, further, to our confessions for doctrinal guidance.

We draw one final statement from the 1982 Report to the General Assembly: **"Let all interpretations be in accord with the rule of love, the two-fold commandment to love God and to love our neighbor."**[9] This principle is so self-evident, we think, that there is no legitimate reason to state something so obvious. But in fact, we need to be reminded again and again in our church that too many debates tempt us to throw out completely these injunctions to love God and neighbor. We are not enveloped in an organization that shows no respect or ready acceptance of those with differing opinions who reach conclusions contrary to ours. Rather, within our church fellowship, at our best, with courtesy and acceptance we listen to and learn from one another.

Many church libraries have a very well received series that has been around for nearly forty years: *The Layman's Bible Commentary*. Many Presbyterians have been exposed to it in whole or in part. In volume 1, *Introduction to the Bible*, the first article by Kenneth J. Foreman asks, "What Is the Bible?"[10] Foreman lists difficulties for the modern Bible reader:

1. the language (Hebrew for the Old Testament and Greek for the New Testament) and the thought forms;
2. that the Bible is oriental (Middle Eastern);

3. the matter of quotations, since there was nothing in the biblical period like our insistence upon precise accrediting of others' words to them or our copyright laws;
4. the figurative, picturesque language, which is often of a poetic nature that presumably was not always intended to be descriptive of reality;
5. that the Bible is literature, that is to say, writings;
6. that it is a unique collection of writings—stories; dramas; chronicles; legends; poems of nature, love, and war; hymns for public and private worship; letters; sermons; biographies; essays—by many people but with a unity of meaning and message.[11]

Not only is there no controversy about these things, but it is quite affirmative for the church that there is such substantial agreement on these things. The detailed definition of Foreman's phrase the "unity of meaning and message"[12] could be explored as there might well be diverse understandings of that view of biblical content. Nevertheless, the point stands: Virtually the entire church has a similar understanding and acceptance of the kinds of issues Foreman lists. It could be tremendously helpful if the whole church could reread such an article, since a great deal of foundational material is covered that permeates so much of our mutual understanding of the Bible.

For what do we turn to the Bible?

Deep issues of faith are, of course, fit subjects for biblical inquiry, and while no one of us would presumably turn to the Bible for specific insights and information about scientific DNA principles, we do anticipate viable perspectives on first causes and the relationship between God and the universe. A "Christian" viewpoint on birth control is not something we expect to find in stories, poems, histories, and biographies centuries old, but we are wise to ascertain how God has worked through history, with a biblical understanding of the causes and nature of history and the human race. We will not be surprised to read different accounts of Israelite history, in the way in which the Promised Land of Israel was conquered, from writers with sometimes conflicting accounts, finding one slant in Joshua and quite another in Judges. We know that police officers typically receive two or three or more eyewitness reports of the same accident, so we search for the message behind what is written as more than one writer gives his or her understanding of an event or of events. Even as we preach and teach in different ways, we unite in the effort that we are making in seeking to communicate in relevant terms the message of a redeeming God of grace and love.

In an overarching manner we collectively turn to the scriptures for the great themes, as we have noted, but also for the great truths that are at the heart of Christianity. Amazingly, again, there is virtual unanimity in our denomination about a whole series of particular parts of the Bible. What Miller called the theme of creation is one that has drawn fascinating interest through the years, including a Bill Moyers series aired on the Public Broadcasting Service as recently as 1996. Prominent Presbyterian attorney William Jennings Bryan, who was almost elected moderator in the 1920s, assisted the prosecution in the famous Scopes trial. Despite creationism talk in recent history, the Presbyterian Church (U.S.A.) now has a far different understanding of the story of God's creation from what was popular in the 1920s.

We concur in knowing and understanding the step-by-step orderliness of creation in the recitations of the two accounts of creation in Genesis. We recognize the God who made the light as being the identical God we know who sent the Light into the world in Jesus Christ. We revel in the gigantic portrayal of a God who is sovereign and almighty and who saw that the world is good. We look up at night into the starlit sky and marvel at the handiwork of a creation that is so lovely to behold, and we gain new insight into the description of the star that led the magi and the pillar of fire that led the Hebrew people through the wilderness by its light at night as the cloud led them by day. We rejoice at the close kinship and intimate relationship between God and God's creatures, and we give thanks that we are made in the image of God. We recognize that the Bible's account of sin, understood as disobedience, rebellion, and a human desire to be all-knowing (and powerful), is terribly real and squarely accurate.

In different years in sometimes remote parts of our world we grasp the fear of heavy rainfall and the coursing gullies that are transformed into floods. Particularly at such times we grope for the reality of genuine dry land when we are soaked and we become convinced that God meant to separate the land from the waters. The glorious arch in the sky surprises us time and time again when we least expect it, so that we almost leap forward to touch the end, even if there is no gold there, since we know that a Creator *is* there. We wonder and shake our heads at the myriad wild flowers in the deserts in the spring, and the number of plants, trees, ferns, and bushes is truly incomprehensible to our small minds. At seed time and at harvest we marvel at the growth process—and then we see a spindly-legged girl blossom into a mature woman while the young man at her side has a voice grown deep—was it just overnight, or was that a dream? They become parents and then we are fully convinced that the greatest miracle of all is birth.

Yes, the creation accounts are ones that unite our finite spirits as we cannot begin to imagine how a Creator could even contemplate such variety, movement, beauty, and glory and then allow us to behold it all.

But this is only the beginning. The sin of disobedience and rebellion quickly becomes greed, hate, murder, deception, trickery, dishonesty, lying, cheating, jealousy, and more evil than we can possibly imagine, but through it all we recognize the truth of it and the reality. We are also aware and convinced that God is not through with us or the universe just yet.

So, the Bible tells us of the sale into Egypt, followed by false accusations, forgotten promises, providence in the form of one who becomes, in fact, the prime minister, and how though others planned it for evil, God made it good. The baby in the bulrushes, the burning bush, Pharaoh's daughter, then plagues, the Passover, and flight follow in rapid fashion. The water is safely crossed—and before long another fording takes place, but in the meantime there is doubt, more rebellion and murmuring, seemingly fruitless wandering, broken vows, anger at how fickle the people are, the mountain, and the commandments, and through it all a covenant kept and a covenant broken. More promises, and finally the resolute challenge, "... but as for me and my household, we will serve the LORD."

Our unanimity in a church in our time in our acceptance of and gratitude for so many instances of grace, mercy, and love truly makes us humble, as all we can really do is sing Hallelujah!

> Break Thou the bread of life,
> Dear Lord, to me,
> As Thou didst break the loaves
> Beside the sea;
> Beyond the sacred page
> I seek Thee, Lord;
> My spirit pants for Thee,
> O living Word!

> Bless Thou the truth, dear Lord,
> Now unto me,
> As Thou didst bless the bread
> By Galilee;
> Then shall all bondage cease,
> All fetters fall;
> And I shall find my peace,
> My all in all.
> (Mary A. Lathbury)[13]

8

Praise the Lord—
and Pass the Peace
Reformed Worship

❖ Many generations of young people have sought to introduce their gullible younger brothers and sisters and neighbors into the glorious endeavor of snipe hunting. They explain carefully that snipe can be caught in an open paper sack, but that snipe are leery of eyes staring at them so the hunter of snipe must wear a covering over the eyes, a blindfold is best, so the snipe will not fear that a search is on and they be caught. So the younger children set out with their paper bags, blindfolded, searching for snipes, and they eventually discover to the glee and jeers of their older "friends" that there is no such thing as a snipe, and that they have wandered in vain looking for something nonexistent.

The search for ties that bind Presbyterians together in the realm of worship will not be a fruitless one, since our common heritage is long and profound. We are impressed once again with the abundance of evidence for an extensive common ground in worship throughout the Presbyterian Church (U.S.A.). Our prevailing similar worship practices are extensive, and the root system for much that we do now extends over four hundred years, so we are not latecomers to the manner in which we approach God and prepare ourselves for being attentive to what God would say to us. How did we arrive at our distinctive destination, and what factors bring us to this place?

We have long been united in our understanding of the centrality of worship in a faithful Christian life. For a vast host of Presbyterians, past and present, no day begins properly without a thoughtful time with scripture and at least a prayer for

God's blessing and guidance of the day. Those who naturally and normally turn to such things as the *Mission Yearbook for Prayer and Study* are wont to include in their prayer time the persons and concerns suggested in that helpful annual material. It is perfectly all right to join the woman who was praying verbally before a small group when she said, "And we pray for all those persons whose names we cannot pronounce." Whether every day begins with private worship time, or not, the church corporately knows that worship is at the very heart of the life of the community. One reason why resistance to change is sometimes apparent is that people have found valid ways for them to be in meaningful relationship with God, and they do not wish to destroy or tamper with such a valuable part of their lives.

The Worship Heritage
from Calvin and Knox

Somewhat surprisingly, John Leith says, "There is no definitive Reformed theology of worship."[1] In view of that fact, why, then, do we often speak about the nature and qualities of Reformed worship? In fact, Presbyterians have developed styles of worship which, over time, have become normative for a congregation. While there may not be a "definitive Reformed theology of worship," there are clear tendencies in worship, and we are all heirs to them all!

One of the earliest things Calvin did in Geneva was to lay out his views of worship—biblically oriented, marked by theological integrity, intelligibility, and simplicity. It was for the edification of the whole Christian community. Calvin provided a form of worship that included written as well as spontaneous prayers. His order began with Psalm 124:8: "Our help is in the name of the LORD, who made heaven and earth."[2]

Calvin was known for placing great stress on the preaching and the teaching of the scriptures, and that biblical orientation meant a central place in worship for the sermon. Worship was theologically oriented in that the place and use of every aspect of worship was tested for its appropriateness in worship. A seminary president who also taught preaching stated over and over again that sermons had to be clearly understood. An illustration was of those members of congregations who would come to him to say something like, "Our pastor ought to teach in your seminary; he is so scholarly, and we do not always know what he is talking about since he is over our heads." The president would say to himself: That is the *last* kind of seminary professor we are looking for! Intelligibility and simplicity were important in Calvin's day, as they are in ours.

According to the rite of 1542, morning worship consisted of two parts: the Liturgy of the Word and the Liturgy of the Upper Room. First:

> *The Liturgy of the Word*
> Scripture Sentence Psalm 124:8
> Confession of Sins
> Prayer for Pardon
> Metrical Psalm
> Collect for Illumination
> Lection
> Sermon[3]

The *Liturgy of the Upper Room* included the collection, intercessions, the Lord's Prayer, Preparation of the Elements (for the Lord's Supper) sung with (the) Apostles' Creed, Words of Institution, Consecration Prayer, Communion with Psalm or Scripture, Post-communion Prayer, Aaronic Blessing.[4]

Although Calvin did not particularly object to using hymns—in fact, he wrote a good many—he stressed the singing of psalms. Several smaller Reformed churches in the United States are still known for singing psalms, as was formerly practiced in the United Presbyterian Church of North America; and singing psalms has long been an emphasis in the Associate Reformed Presbyterian Church. The early Reformers interpreted the Second Commandment almost literally: "You shall not make for yourself an idol [the King James version reads "graven images"], whether in the form of anything that is in heaven above, or that is on the earth beneath. . . . You shall not bow down to them or worship them; for I the LORD your God am a jealous God" (Ex. 20:4–5a).

Unlike Luther, Calvin insisted on scriptural justification for all the elements of worship. Images were forbidden, as were ostentatious displays of any kind of worship. It was felt that even viewing statues, paintings, and other artistic presentations could lead to idolatry. A number of the Reformed cathedrals had been constructed for Roman Catholic worship; images were removed from them, but the magnificent stained glass windows were not removed. How hard it must have been for Zwingli, for instance, a talented and capable musician, to insist that the organ in the great cathedral in Zurich, where he was pastor, had to be dismantled, but he did so.

While icons of various kinds have traditionally been identified with the Orthodox churches, and while crucifixes and holy relics for veneration have held fascination and reality for many within the Roman Catholic Church, the early Reformed custom and practice was to leave sanctuaries without adornment. For several centuries, an almost austere worship experience was common for Reformed Christians.

The Directory for Worship

At times Calvin gave the definition of where a (true) church is: wherever the word is faithfully preached and the sacraments properly administered. All else is secondary. Presbyterians have believed that God takes the initiative, and chapter I in the Directory for Worship (the second part of the *Book of Order*) is explicit in naming two obvious places where God has acted, in creation and in covenant. Thus, regardless of relatively minor variations from place to place, we all join in stressing several necessary ingredients in worship. Presbyterians from even quite distant places feel at home in almost any

Presbyterian worship service. We are bound together with six foundational elements.

1. Prayer

Regardless of the nature of the gathering, and before serious conversation begins on any subject, all parts of the church routinely and appropriately begin with prayer, often very earnest prayer. It is not surprising that chapter II in the Directory for Worship, titled "The Elements of Christian Worship," begins with prayer. Several kinds of prayer are mentioned briefly: adoration, thanksgiving, confession, supplication, intercession, and self-dedication. There is nothing particularly distinctive about Presbyterians and prayer, but we do not always recognize that we are held together in very profound ways such as in basic elements like prayer in the spiritual life development and nurture of individuals and of the whole church.

2. The Sermon

While prayer may be little different from one mainline denomination to another, solid biblical preaching is distinctively Presbyterian. Presbyterian preachers do not deliver homilies; they proclaim the good news in Jesus Christ, using scripture as the foundation. Presbyterian sermons are often those which exegete (that is, mine the text word by word, or phrase by phrase, or section by section) passages of scripture, in turn. Presbyterians prepare their sermons with care.

The use of the lectionary for preaching increasingly is found in Presbyterian churches. One advantage is obvious; another is rarely mentioned. The obvious boon is that the preacher who tends to ride a "hobby horse" subject to death is encouraged—not forced—to choose one or more of the established lectionary passages each week, thus covering a much wider variety of biblical materials over a period of time, and keeping up with the ecclesiastical seasons. The other more hidden benefit for the preacher is the opportunity and privilege to study the weekly passages with other like-minded lectionary users in the area, regardless of denomination, since all use virtually the same lectionary. Greater sensitivities and insights are provided than what might be obtained in individual study, and the ecumenical relationships developed in joint Bible study can be of great importance for the individuals concerned. Some ministers review the weekly Bible passages with persons within their own congregations, and that can benefit everyone who participates. The *Book of Common Worship* notes:

> When the sixteenth-century Reformers rejected the use of the lectionary in use in the medieval church, they did not reject the notion that the selection of Bible readings for use in worship should be disciplined and informed by the wisdom of the church. Instead of the medieval lectionary, the Reformers recovered an ancient tradition of reading and preaching through the books of the Bible in course. This principle of selection of scripture passages is called . . . continuous reading as distinct from the principle of . . . select reading in which particular readings are always assigned for specific days.[5]

3. The Sacraments

It is virtually impossible for a Presbyterian to locate a Presbyterian church anywhere in the land where he or she does not feel at home for the celebration of the Lord's Supper, even to the manner of celebration, whether it be by the method of passing the trays of bread and cup down the rows of pews, or more like some other denominations whereby the entire congregation goes forward to be served. Baptisms are also quite similar throughout the church. The sacraments, and the way we celebrate them, are not "the glue which holds us together," but they are certainly reminders of our common ties.

Reformed practice on inclusion, not exclusion, at the table of the Lord is distinctive. The citation in the Directory for Worship is worth noting. "All the baptized faithful are to be welcomed to the Table, and none shall be excluded because of race, sex, age, economic status, social class, handicapping condition, difference of culture or language, or any barrier created by human injustice." The community nature of the Christian family is explicitly fully endorsed for this central occasion in worship.[6]

4. The Liturgy

One of the great privileges and joys that the itinerant preacher has is to partake of magnificent worship services and experiences throughout the width and length of the denomination, and to know that the visitor is "at home." People with imagination and creativity in small churches and large, in conference centers and in governing bodies, are planning and leading extremely meaningful and thrilling services of worship. Anyone who thinks the Presbyterian Church (U.S.A.) is on its last legs has not had the utter glorious advantages of sampling the richness and variety of ways in which God is being praised, glorified, and worshiped in our church. No two presbytery worship services are any longer the same, and one facet of this trend is the careful planning that goes into congregational, governing body, college chapel, conference center, and home worship. This is a cause for great rejoicing!

5. Offerings

The Directory for Worship makes scant reference to the offering of tithes and gifts, but giving is central to the Christian's response to what God has done.[7] Two special offerings are symbols of what unites Presbyterians. The first is the Joy Offering, normally received at Christmastime, which is designated (1) for racial ethnic schools and colleges; and (2) to assist retired church personnel who are in particular need. The other is the One Great Hour of Sharing Offering, which is ordinarily received at Eastertime, to help meet emergencies and unusual exigencies related to natural disasters such as floods, tornadoes, or earthquakes, or for refugees made homeless by political eruptions or wars. We join forces to offer aid to those who are in need of special kinds of assistance.

6. *Newer practices*

Such things as healing services and anointing with oil, which in some cases are old traditions in the Church universal, are, nevertheless, new to many Presbyterians. Yet there are comments about these things and other worship practices and styles in the current Directory for Worship.

Reforming Reformed Worship!

It has been put starkly: grow old and die, or grow young and thrive. Growing old describes not just the chronologically gifted, though that is a part of the subject, but the notion some churches have of keeping without change the same style of worship that has been the tradition in a particular church since Noah's flood. Likewise, growing young does not mean the age of a church in a particular location, but it does mean having meaningful worship and preaching for, and attracting, as a result, the young in age, and those of any age who are seeking genuine refreshment for their souls.

Some are suggesting that the noble and well-intentioned effort to keep up with the times by having some guitar music and Praise Singers with a modern beat to the music is well and good, but that the primary appeal of such efforts is to baby boomers only. Baby boomers feel more comfortable in singing Christian songs that have been composed by and for their generation. That kind of blended service combining traditional hymns and music with new words and more popular music has its place, but neither kind of music and worship speaks to Generation X, the children of the baby boomers, we are told. Each session will need to do its own exploration of this vital topic.

If the church is to grow by attracting today's young people, a session, pastor, and people must make significant reflection, and perhaps major adjustments in music, preaching, and in all of worship. It is said that Generation X people do not think (or sing) in linear fashion. Rather, the lyrics need to be repeated instead of being linear since younger people do not absorb the message unless there is repetition. Further, the songs must use the language of the heart, affecting the emotions, with less resort to reasoning and the intellect for communication. If the church is serious about its task of evangelism, its worship styles, and especially its music, must be the kind that find resonance with a new generation with a different sort of worship background and absorption possibility. Perhaps the current popularity of the old hymn "Amazing Grace" is indicative of a tie between some older gospel-type singing and what appeals to today's Generation X.

The issue then becomes: Is it necessary for Reformed worship to change, or be reformed, for the worthy purposes of both evangelism and nurture? If only dynamic change will attract youth, what does a congregation do to keep the middle age group and the senior citizens who love "the old hymns"? Really, the question is: Does Reformed worship, if it exists at all, have special ingredients that together form a kind of worship experience that can ultimately have appeal and virtue for all, or is Reformed worship truly a kind of worship, by definition, which can and does change with such things as culture, nationality, sometimes race, idiom, age, and style?

As we are one in many other aspects of worship, we are surely one church in bumping up against a social reality that has never faced us previously, at least not in this major dimension of a cultural pattern which seems pervasive. Challenges await us on every side, but none more difficult, and perhaps determinative, than of what each session decides is the best way to witness to the various age groups and cultural mores that face us.

One of the joys and benefits of being part of a much larger ecumenical Christian fellowship is seeing and learning what kinds of worship are being used in other churches and countries. There is no question about the enrichment that comes to those of us in the Reformed family of churches from others in different traditions. The Roman Catholic monk Thomas Merton has provided a sense of meditation and oneness with God that has been richly rewarding for Protestants as well as for other Roman Catholics. The Dutch priest Henri Nouwen and the French priest Michel Quoist have greatly influenced a generation with their prayers, insights, and meditations. The Taizé Community has given invaluable resources to the whole Christian community in the world with printed liturgies, litanies, hymns, and prayers.

But these individuals and this one group are just the beginning of the world Christian community that has shaped Reformed worship in recent decades; we shall never be the same. There is rarely an ecumenical gathering anywhere in the world that does not produce new hymns, worship emphases, and topics to explore that incrementally change every participant, to be sure, but the entire constituency, as resources resonate among those who receive them secondhand. The thematic expositions at ecumenical gatherings are frequently germinal and lead to innovative developments in theology and worship. The beauty for the Reformed community is obvious. As people who are open to change—call it reformation—Presbyterians are always looking for better and more creative ways to worship God and to sing praises, and, in turn, to be addressed by God through God's chosen spokespersons. As an organization, Presbyterian Women, especially, invite leaders from all over the globe to their meetings for just such inspiration and insights through creative worship.

The Directory for Worship states, "The Church has always experienced a tension between form and freedom in worship. . . . The Presbyterian Church (U.S.A.) acknowledges that all forms of worship are provisional and subject to reformation."[8]

The Book of Common Worship

The revised 1993 *Book of Common Worship* is greatly expanded from previous editions, but like the other earlier ones, this *Book of Common Worship* is not official, that is, its use is not required in Presbyterian churches. This book does, however, contain a wealth of worship resources that can be mined by pastors and sessions and other church members who may vary considerably in their worship practices. The Sunday lectionary passages in the *Presbyterian Planning Calendar* and the daily Bible readings in the *Mission Yearbook for Prayer and Study* are both listed in the *Book of Common Worship* lectionary section, for instance. The rich resources include many suggested scripture verses for such use as a call to worship in a public worship service, as well as prayers for virtually every imaginable purpose in worship, public and private—even prayers by such persons as Christina Rossetti, John Henry Newman, Dag Hammarskjöld, Howard Thurman, and Augustine of Hippo. The worthwhile and helpful information and material for worship seem to go on and on, but that leads to the one negative of this magnificent tome: it is heavy. Some worship leaders will make copies of materials to be used on a particular occasion for easier use. There is an electronic version, so any portion of the contents can be printed out as needed for each service or other desired use.

The Presbyterian Hymnal

The 1990 *The Presbyterian Hymnal* has been far more popular than anyone had any reason to expect. Once again, our hymnal brings together those churches whose sessions have selected this excellent worship resource. To a far greater extent than any previously published in our church, the *Hymnal* includes both tunes and words from worshiping communities far beyond our shores so that it is ecumenical in a marvelous fashion. Recent hymns, as well as the standard hymns of the centuries, are found in this volume, but no attempt was made to add anything like the "Orders for the Public Worship of God," which were in the 1972 *Worshipbook*.

The Directory for Worship has gone through another revision recently, and the church has agreed that it is superb, and those mandatory sections are, with few exceptions, in force. The place of prayer, preaching, the sacraments, and the liturgy are momentous in the life of our church, even as the style of such things also changes in ways designed to relate to people as we face the next era. Probably nothing has changed so much as has our music, and we can hardly be inaccurate by saying that further change is bound to come, and come soon. We *are* always reforming.

Finally, the worship resources and the charting of a direction in corporate worship practice are all in place so that we are unusually well prepared to face the future, and to adjust as may be appropriate. Thanks be to God!

> God of our life, through all the circling years,
>   We trust in Thee;
> In all the past, through all our hopes and fears,
>   Thy hand we see.
> With each new day, when morning lifts the veil,
> We own Thy mercies, Lord, which never fail.
>
> God of the past, our times are in Thy hand;
>   With us abide.
> Lead us by faith to hope's true promised land;
>   Be Thou our guide.
> With Thee to bless, the darkness shines as light,
> And faith's fair vision changes into sight.
>
> God of the coming years, through paths unknown
>   We follow Thee;
> When we are strong, Lord, leave us not alone;
>   Our refuge be.
> Be Thou for us in life our daily bread,
> Our heart's true home when all our years have sped.
>   (Hugh Thomson Kerr)[9]

9

After "Go, Therefore . . ."

Our Mission Challenge

This is a multiple-choice quiz. Choose your answer before reading on—and no cheating! The first action of the first General Assembly of the Presbyterian Church in this country in 1789 in Philadelphia was to: (a) urge the Congress, then in session in New York, to provide pensions for those soldiers who were wounded in the Revolutionary War; (b) adopt the Westminster Confession with the Larger and Shorter Catechisms; (c) send missionaries to the frontier; or (d) agree that every session could send one elder to each meeting of its presbytery.

You probably discerned, in a chapter on mission, that the third response listed above is the right one.[1] Our church in this country did not begin with stating its own rights, or even debating theology, but looked outward in mission. That fact reminds us of the moderator of the 207th General Assembly (1995), Marj Carpenter, who said the church needed to concentrate on three things: Mission, Mission, and Mission!

In this connection, it is important to note that at the very first meeting of what became the Presbyterian Church in the United States, in 1861, Southerners also declared mission to be the great end of Christ's church.[2]

In previous chapters we have sought to name several subjects that we have hoped that readers might remember. In this chapter we are bunching the issues succinctly. First, the PC(USA) in its very being has endorsed and made abundantly clear its commitment to mission. Second, current mission challenges, though in a different manner, are just as daunting and demanding as in an earlier time. Third, we urge continued support for PC(USA) mission: (a) through prayer for new ventures; (b) through generous giving; and (c) through challenging the best personnel to become engaged in vital mission. Before reviewing the entire church's commitment to mission in this country first, and then overseas, two things should be noted. The good news is that the mission pages in our church's history book are glorious with a never-ending stream of heroes and heroines, both those who have left hearth and home and those who have served in so many ways while never leaving Hometown, U.S.A.

The bad news is that as a church we have sometimes been in mission with motives and techniques that have not been appropriate—at least from the perspective of splendid hindsight. In his book on the world mission of Presbyterians, G. Thompson Brown correctly wrote that in some cases our proselytizing had the wrong motives, the wrong methods, and the wrong results. Brown says, "Gandhi criticized 'missionary proselytizing' as being done for 'ulterior motives' with a 'commercial aspect.' . . . There is a danger that in the doing of mission we appeal to the superiority of Western civilization and our advanced technology. Christianity in China was so closely identified with the colonial system that patriotic Chinese made the charge: 'Win a convert, lose a citizen.'"[3]

Not to belabor the point, but to show that Brown is not alone in frankly declaring the "bad news" about the great mission enterprise, see the repeated observations made by eyewitnesses of the mission thrust in Latin America in H. McKennie Goodpasture's book *Cross and Sword*, which recounts the sad spectacle of forced conversions and other evils.[4] Improper motives and methods were used as the gospel spread to the western frontier in this country. And it has not been just Christians who have exploited persons, particularly among Native Americans and African Americans, but business persons, politicians, and plain ordinary citizens headed West have often shown the worst of oppression, chicanery, and the lust for power and wealth.[5]

The good news is that despite our human mistakes and

shortcomings God has gloriously blessed the labors of this people of God. "The Reformed tradition and mainstream Protestantism shared a concern for education that produced an extensive network of colleges and universities prior to the Civil War. By 1860, 175 of the 182 colleges had been founded by churches or through denominational initiatives, and Presbyterians led the way with 49."[6] Today there are 66 of these colleges related to our denomination in the United States. Untold thousands of faculty and students have been influenced by the gospel message in these institutions through the years. Our church is now related to over 400 educational institutions in other countries, not including the teachers we appoint through the Amity Foundation to teach in China!

In some of our partner churches in Africa there is an *annual* growth of 15 percent, with our mission coworkers assisting. The health workers, primary school teachers, and agricultural extension workers of our partner churches in that region view the sharing of their Christian faith as an integral part of their work. After the Chinese government allowed the first church to be reopened in 1979, an average of two churches have been reopened or established in China every three days, and the beat goes on. There are more Presbyterians in Korea than there are in the Presbyterian Church (U.S.A.); our denomination was the human instrument for beginning Presbyterian work in Korea in 1884. Korean churches are the fastest growing ones in the Presbyterian Church (U.S.A.) in this country.

In 1996, six thousand youth and adults—the maximum number possible—attended the five youth conferences at the Montreat Conference Center in North Carolina. The new national youth program, the Presbyterian Youth Connection, is being met with widespread enthusiasm. The new Pentecost Offering is being designated for youth and young adult ministry and for children at risk.

HungryHearts News is approaching 5,000 readers eager to learn more about spiritual formation. Anyone who believes that mission zeal in the Presbyterian Church (U.S.A.) is lagging does not know one amazing statistic: Every year some

4,000 people express an interest in serving overseas or in this country in mission with the Worldwide Ministries Division. Some 1,000 applications for service are sent annually and several hundred appointments for short- or long-term positions are made. Our longtime commitment as a denomination to mission is alive and well through such demonstrations as these.

The whole church is challenged today to reflect theologically and biblically about what we can learn from the past as we see new horizons and confront new opportunities in the next millennium. It is essential to keep in mind that in the early days of mission by and through the Presbyterian Church there was no distinction between national and foreign mission—in those days the ever-expanding frontier was "foreign," at least to those who continued to reside "back East." The *Mission Yearbook for Prayer and Study*, begun in 1883, seeks to provide information, listing needs for prayer in both the United States and overseas.

What are some of the lessons about mission that we have learned? First and foremost, that the mission is not our mission, but God's mission. Then, that the church in each place, usually called the national church, is the primary bearer of the gospel in that culture. The gospel is most effective when it is preached in the idiom and in the accent of that culture and language. Foreign missionaries can normally help most by playing a supporting role, not by being the lead actor. We have also learned that mission and unity belong together, and we shall note later how that principle has long been most significant for Presbyterian mission. There is no reason to seek to perpetuate American denominationalism across other national boundaries.

At our peril we sometimes forget what most of us know deep inside our hearts, whether our mission be in Anytown, U.S.A., or the most distant outpost across the globe: Evangelism and social justice are two sides of the same coin. We do not present the full gospel unless and until we demonstrate both issues. Again, regardless of location, on a reservation in the southwestern United States or in eastern Asia, we aid no one in denigrating another's culture and religion. Respect for people and their cultures and religions is essential for mission. Jesus ate, traveled, and worked with persons of all kinds of backgrounds, and he seemed particularly at home with the poor. His words in both Matthew 25 and Luke 4 are powerful as he taught about ministry with the oppressed, the hungry, the thirsty, the naked, the sick, and the stranger.

One lesson was learned most forcefully in India in the Punjab area, where over 150 years ago missionaries went to the best educated in the most formal language, but such tactics went nowhere. *Then,* speaking the native Punjabi among the lowest class, or outcasts, telling about a Christ who came to the lame, the lost, and to free the oppressed—as these outcasts were—the gospel of liberation brought families, then extended families, then entire villages to Christ and the church! In the Punjabi language the word for "oppressed" that Jesus used in Luke 4, quoted from Isaiah 61:1–2a, means "the outcasts, or persons of no caste." Response from the poorest of the poor: That's who we are! Jesus came for us!

Mission to the poor, whether in Chicago or Cairo, is our challenge and our opportunity. Except to get their votes and to be customers for drugs, few Americans seem to be greatly interested in the poor. In the past, as a church we have been with them *on occasion.* What is our church address now?

To turn to another pattern of thinking, in the past we have had a fairly easy task in relating to non-Presbyterians because we have been in the driver's seat, along with other mainline church folk, socially, politically, economically, and culturally. It is a different day. Mayors, bankers, brokers, industrialists, school teachers, physicians, and managers were our Presbyterian constituencies. But there are reputedly more Muslims in the United States today than Presbyterians—or Episcopalians! Historically, dating back to the spread of Islam through the Middle East, across north Africa, and into Europe, and most memorably, in the Crusades, Christians have had an adversarial relationship to Islam and its adherents, Muslims. Muslims need a first-rate public relations expert at the least, we think, because their media coverage has been so poor, if not outright hostile. If we take seriously the Confession of 1967, what about concentrating on some decent form of reconciliation with a group in the Middle East, where Presbyterians historically have had more mission work than any other denomination, especially as so many of these friends are now our next-door neighbors?

At the height of tension and Presbyterian awareness when Presbyterian missionary Ben Weir was being held hostage in Lebanon, his magnificent wife, Carol, was pleading for our understanding of Muslims and what they were trying to say to us! Surely, it is not only when terror and violence come to the fore that we need to learn about Islam—and Hinduism and Buddhism—and such things as overt hostile nationalism through study, and to ask why events are taking place, and begin to prepare to act responsibly. In short, *the time is now* to witness—and learn—with persons of other faiths, or religious groupings, as well as with those who profess no religion.

National Mission:
Westward Ho! and Texas, Too

Despite the initial action of the Presbyterian General Assembly in 1789 concerning mission to the frontier, it was not until 1837 that the denomination (technically, the Old School General Assembly) created a Board of Foreign Missions, which originally included what came to be called national, or home, missions.

The first action of the Presbyterian Church in the United States in supporting mission has been mentioned, and it should also be noted that the United Presbyterian Church of North America had a profound effect through its efforts to organize and support schools for minority persons, especially African Americans in the south. Many current church leaders have come through such institutions as the rural schools in Wilcox County, Alabama; Boggs Academy in Georgia (now under different auspices); and Knoxville College, Knoxville, Tennessee. Stillman College in Tuscaloosa, Alabama, was sponsored by the Presbyterian Church in the United States primarily for African American students. Warren Wilson College in Swannanoa, North Carolina, is a Presbyterian college for mountain and minority students, and for many foreign students who need to work at the college to help defray the costs of their education.

Menaul School in Albuquerque, New Mexico, shared with those attending the General Assembly in that city in 1996 what our support there through the years has meant for minorities in that area, primarily those of Hispanic and Native American ancestry.

The Labor Temple and the East Harlem Protestant Parish in New York were still another type of mission outreach, commonly known then as settlement houses and found in places like Detroit and Chicago and in other big cities. They were—and many others still are—multipurpose places of refuge, education, and recreation, providing such things as job training in poor neighborhoods.

Some of the great national missionaries whose ministries still shine in the Presbyterian Church (U.S.A.) today were:

1. David Brainerd. The saga of David Brainerd has been told and retold through the years. This man dedicated his life to mission work with Native Americans, especially the Delawares. Even when he was dying of tuberculosis, he crossed the "howling wilderness" to minister to Native Americans then located between the Delaware and Susquehanna Rivers. For many years he was the missionary par excellence as he forgot himself in service to his Lord.[7]

2. Sheldon Jackson, for whom a college in Sitka, Alaska, was named, was an unusual national missionary. Jackson organized one church after another in nine states and three territories in the prairie and mountain regions, even reaching to the southwest, before going to Alaska. It is thrilling to go through the western states and learn of the numerous churches that trace their founding to Sheldon Jackson. William

Warren Sweet writes, "During one period of 16 days he formed 7 churches. . . . [T]he Department of the Interior authorized him to establish a public school system for the territory (of Alaska)."[8] Probably no other missionary in history left the kind of record that he did, since he was an inveterate photographer. No better collection exists than of his early photos of Native Americans.

3. Donaldina Cameron. Like Jackson, Donaldina Cameron has an institution named for her, in her case in San Francisco, where she established a settlement house that sheltered young Chinese, mostly women, who were ill-treated by men in the wild early days of that city. It is not surprising that a Presbyterian church in the Chinatown of San Francisco and an all-purpose community center thrive today under Chinese American leadership and direction.

4. E. O. Guerrant was physician, minister, and synod evangelist for several years. No institution was named for this pioneer in bringing Christ to the people of the Appalachian mountains, but a presbytery was. For many years Guerrant Presbytery in the Presbyterian Church in the United States included the churches and the area in the mountains where he had done itinerant work, holding meetings and revivals, establishing Sunday schools, and serving as a doctor along the way. He was devoted to "mountain work," even raising money in places like New York for the work.[9] The presbytery bearing his name has been subsumed into Transylvania Presbytery.

5. Dr. Marcus Whitman and Mrs. Narcissa Prentiss Whitman, and Henry H. Spalding and Eliza Hart Spalding. Mrs. Whitman and Mrs. Spalding were the first white women to cross the Rocky Mountains, on July 4, 1836, riding sidesaddle, and they were the first white women many Native Americans in the Northwest had ever seen. Neither woman ever returned home. The Whitman wagon was the first to travel through southern Idaho and into what is now Boise. The Spaldings served in Lapwai, Idaho, and the Whitmans went on to Walla Walla, Washington, to work among the Cayuse Indians. Not an institution nor a presbytery, but the town of Spalding,

Idaho, was named for those early missionaries among the Nez Percé tribe. The Whitmans aided in the settlement of Washington and Oregon, but they were eventually murdered by those among whom they worked, who believed that a serious epidemic had been brought by the eastern doctor.[10]

Other, less well-known, missionaries established schools and colleges, as well as churches, in the South, Southwest, and all across the West and into Alaska and Hawaii. There were many patterns. In 1911 Charles Cook was instrumental in founding what is now known as Cook College and Theological School, for Native Americans, in Tucson, Arizona; it is now located in Tempe, Arizona. Pan American School in Kingsville, Texas, has provided quality high school education for over seventy years for Presbyterian Hispanics, the children of Presbyterian pastors in Mexico, and other students from countries in Latin America. Many churches throughout the western United States were offshoots of older, more established churches, and some were brought to life through specific decisions made by the Board of National Missions in New York, or through extension-minded presbyteries and then synods. Because of the great distances involved in relating to older established churches in the East, Presbyterians in the West often felt much more isolated than those in the East.

It should be noted that in many parts of the country during the era of the great western settlement there was often direct competition between Roman Catholics and Protestants, a part of our history of which none of us should be proud. The climate has changed for the better, amazingly, particularly since Vatican II, so that there is excellent cooperation and joint mission efforts are found in many areas, particularly in social service, human rights, and peace issues.

Few changes in recent years have been so marked as the shift in the center of operation in national mission to virtually every congregation, which sees itself as a base for mission. Some degree of coordination has been lost, but the participation of so many church members in mission is a sight to behold. In contrast to the recent past, members can now see with their own eyes both what they are doing physically themselves, as well as what is being done locally with their mission contributions. One startling change is in the concept of the phrase "national missionary." The majority of "missionaries" in this country today are not paid, full-time, and lifelong career persons, but those who volunteer for a much shorter time working in a project. The most popular volunteer post today in the United States is at first surprising until a little thought is given. Work done there is legitimate—it needs to be done; the variety of work means that persons with many skills can participate, from teachers and librarians, and houseparents, to builders, mechanics, gardeners, and computer experts; many people of various ethnic backgrounds are helped. The place is Sheldon Jackson College in Sitka, Alaska. Volunteers enjoy serving students in a place where Native Americans live, a place where many volunteers had not visited previously. But in an age when information is so vast, we are called upon to teach students how to use information technologies to solve problems.

Other attractions for part-time assistance are in the national and regional parks. More difficult and wearing assignments for volunteers and professionals are where they have been for generations, but with differences: the inner cities. The problems are often mammoth, and few claim to be able to provide the answers to those problems; serious and vital challenges await the church.

At all levels of the church today various groups are seeking ways to deal constructively with a whole range of issues: inadequate and dilapidated housing; the fallout from "welfare reform"; unwed teenage mothers; drug addiction; racism and related issues; the families of the imprisoned, in addition to those behind bars themselves; unemployment and underemployment; school dropouts; adequate and fairly delivered medical systems; activities and homes for older people; crisis counseling centers—the list seems almost endless. The hopeful note, though, is the vast number of those searching for appropriate responses to this wide range of issues at the congregational, presbytery, synod, and General Assembly levels.

However Presbyterians may feel about ordaining homosexuals, increasing numbers are concerned with ensuring fair and just treatment for gays and lesbians in all walks of life. It is a rare Presbyterian congregation that is not engaged in one or many ministries of compassion, seeking to meet human need. If we have ever been bound together in one great national mission, that time is now! "All one body, we."

In the nineteenth century a Presbyterian Hospital was established in many cities around the country. Today a whole new congregational-based health ministry is developing. The parish nurse is becoming increasingly common as we emphasize preventive rather than curative medicine.

Global Mission:
The Biblical Mandate to "Go"

In 1837 the General Assembly (the Old School Assembly) organized a Board of Foreign Missions, and by whatever name at the denominational level, the church has been sending missionaries abroad ever since. As we approach the next millennium, our church is related to strong witnessing partners in eighty countries, and during the last decade the numerical majority of the world's Christians has shifted from North America and Europe to Asia, Africa, and Latin America!

In our culture we idolize the sports heroine and hero, as well as the darling of pop culture. If we are searching for heroines and heroes in mission, we need to bypass the missionaries of our church and focus on nationals who often face true hardships and hazards within their own countries. It is all right, though, to recognize a few from our denomination who have achieved notable ends.

1. John Livingstone Nevius. For forty years Nevius was a missionary in China, but he is best known for his principles of missionary endeavor, which were practiced most spectacularly in Korea. Headed for a furlough in 1889, Nevius was invited to stop in Korea to share his "plan" that he had developed as an itinerant evangelist and theological seminary professor in China. The principles are simple, but powerful:

1. Self-propagation. Each believer should teach someone.
2. Self-government. Every group should be under
   its unpaid leaders; circuits under their own paid
   helpers.
3. Self-support. As soon as it is founded, each group
   should begin paying toward the current helper's
   salary. No pastor would receive foreign funds.
   Tithing was taught.
4. Systematic Bible study for every believer.[11]

2. Robert E. Speer. In 1891, Dr. Speer was called to be a
Board Secretary in New York while still a student at Princeton
Seminary; he served until his retirement in 1937. He was the
best-known missionary spokesperson of his time and moderator of the General Assembly in 1927. No one of his generation
visited, under often extremely difficult traveling situations, so
many lands, nor so many mission posts; he was a dynamic
speaker, administrative innovator, and mission thinker. He
helped Board missionaries, Board members and the entire
church to look to the future. Each missionary felt that Dr.
Speer had personally recruited her or him to that person's
special assignment.[12]
    3. William H. Sheppard. An African American, William
Sheppard integrated the Presbyterian mission in the Belgian
Congo, now Zaire, when he and Samuel N. Lapsley were the
founders of the mission. After the untimely death of Lapsley,
William M. Morrison and Sheppard worked together. Sheppard was a double anomaly. His own church, the Presbyterian
Church in the United States, did not accord him the respect
and position that it gave Morrison or Lapsley. Further, the
PCUS did not endorse any involvement in politics, but Lapsley and Sheppard wrote and spoke about the inhuman treatment of Africans at the hands of the functionaries of King
Leopold of Belgium. The chief sin of the Africans was they did
not produce rubber rapidly enough. Mark Twain in this country and the parliament in Great Britain joined in the outcry
over the manner in which Africans were treated as slave la-

borers liable to have their hands cut off for certain offenses. For his courageous work Sheppard was made a fellow of the Royal Geographical Society in England.[13]

4. Pearl S. Buck. Controversial, if nothing else, Pearl Buck was born of Presbyterian missionaries and grew up in China. She was later a Presbyterian missionary herself who came to disagree fundamentally with many of the policies of the Board. Her highly acclaimed book *The Good Earth* made her famous, and she did not want to harm the work of the Board, so she resigned. There were those who thought that she should have been fired! She was very close to many rural and agrarian Chinese, and she took their part both in person and in her writings.[14]

Note of Urgency:
Mission Now

There is urgency about mission today. The role that volunteers can play has never been more significant, since help is needed in all kinds of places. There is unprecedented human suffering; totalitarian regimes are more skilled at torturing people than King Leopold was in the Belgian Congo. More lethal weapons wound more people, and racial prejudice and discrimination, while seeming more genteel, are still virulent around the world. Bombings in New York, Oklahoma City, Atlanta, and elsewhere are beginning to seem almost expected. The future of places like Hong Kong is uncertain as drastic changes are taking place in the transfer of political power from the British to China. As the population grows by leaps and bounds at over 3 percent annually in several countries in Africa and in places like Pakistan, there is inadequate decent housing and squalid conditions still prevail in many places. Non-Christian religions have had a renaissance throughout the Middle East and in parts of Europe and Asia.

The reality is, of course, that even if we wished never to send another mission coworker or mission volunteer beyond the shores of the United States, global mission would still be upon us. Like it or not, globalization is a fact of life. Only in relatively isolated parts of the United States is a Muslim mosque or Buddhist temple not visible. The only question that remains is the extent to which we choose to greet adherents of other world religions and whether we wish to welcome immigrants to our communities. Can we find those who work on or own large farms where no grain or other products are shipped overseas? The Internet is worldwide, and we can communicate instantaneously with most major cities. Business of all kinds can no longer be limited to our country alone. American tourists are known the world over, and foreign students are in virtually every American college and certainly in each university of our land. We live in a global village in a global economy with global communications and global political intrusions into our lives daily. The church today has an unparalleled opportunity to show hospitality and to be neighborly with people from many countries around the world and to witness to the world community without ever leaving home!

All of that means tremendous opportunities and challenges, but no one foresees an easy time of it. While the challenge is daunting, the potential difficulties are enormous; the world is changing so fast that the very notion of long-range planning seems archaic. God is surely not through with us yet, so the tradition continues!

The Presbyterian Center in Louisville is now being referred to as "The National Resource Center" by the General Assembly Council. The new name is intended to identify more accurately what 100 Witherspoon St., Louisville, Kentucky, is for the Presbyterian Church (U.S.A.). One reason for moving offices from Atlanta and New York to Louisville was to try to change the negative image of being out of touch that was given to the denominational agencies in those previous places. The National Resource Center may continue to reap the wrath of some, but every effort is being made to unify the Presbyterian Church (U.S.A.) through an emphasis on providing services for the denomination, particularly for congregations, and to respond appropriately to actions of the General Assembly.

Just by turning the pages of this book a person can be reminded of how closely our church has been related to all aspects of life in this country and around the world. The tradition continues. We are united together with our "national resource center" so that Presbyterians can make a difference for Christ in the world of the twenty-first century as we have in the nineteenth and twentieth centuries. None of us knows all of the contours of the twenty-first century, but we do know God intends that Presbyterians be active in shaping that world in accord with the values and the hope of the gospel.

Thus the divisions of the General Assembly Council are providing leadership for a variety of ministry initiatives. The Congregational Ministries Division is developing fresh resources to enable the Presbyterian Church of the twenty-first century to experience spiritual renewal, to be energized for support of the whole mission of the church, and to reach out to youth and young adults—the church's future. The National Ministries Division is seeking to lead the church in a new emphasis on evangelism and church development, in fresh ministries of justice, and in building partnerships between all of the congregations, governing bodies, and institutions of the church. The Worldwide Ministries Division reminds us that the task of global evangelism is far from completed. That division seeks to equip us to join with partner churches throughout the world in preaching the gospel, building up the church, healing the sick, educating the next generation, and receiving spiritual gifts from Christians across the globe.

We have been deeply involved in mission throughout our history. Today there are people ready and willing to serve. The church now needs to be engaged in prayerful support for mission and to be equally forthcoming in financially supporting mission.

So—we highlight again the fundamental issues for this chapter on mission:

1. **The Presbyterian Church (U.S.A.) has had, and now has, a firm commitment to mission in which we all share.**

2. **In various ways, the entire church supports the worldwide mission of the church.**

3. **Each of us needs to provide continuing support for mission through prayer and generous giving and through the challenging of our best people, young and old, to consider seriously mission service.**

Lord, you give the great commission:
"Heal the sick and preach the word."
Lest the church neglect its mission,
And the gospel go unheard,
Help us witness to your purpose
With renewed integrity;
With the Spirit's gifts empower us
For the work of ministry.

Lord, you call us to your service:
"In my name baptize and teach."
That the world may trust your promise,
Life abundant meant for each,
Give us all new fervor, draw us
Closer in community;
With the Spirit's gifts empower us
For the work of ministry.

Lord you make the common holy:
"This my body, this my blood."
Let us all, for earth's true glory,
Daily lift life heavenward,
Asking that the world around us
Share your children's liberty;
With the Spirit's gifts empower us
For the work of ministry.

Lord, you show us love's true measure:
"Father, what they do, forgive."
Yet we hoard as private treasure
All that you so freely give.
May your care and mercy lead us
To a just society;
With the Spirit's gifts empower us
For the work of ministry.

Lord, you bless with words assuring:
"I am with you to the end."
Faith and hope and love restoring,
May we serve as you intend,
And, amid the cares that claim us,
Hold in mind eternity;
With the Spirit's gifts empower us
For the work of ministry.
                                    (Jeffery W. Rowthorn)[15]

10

St. John's-by-the-Gas-Station
The Particular Church

For many years, Yale Divinity School professor Halford Luccock had a regular column in *The Christian Century*. For his witty reference to the particular church, his illustration was a hypothetical church by the gas station. Not all of our churches can be so easily located by a well-known landmark.

Reference has been made to the pivotal report of the Commission of 1925 in the Presbyterian Church in the U.S.A., but one facet of that report is not well-known. The report stated, and the Assembly agreed, that the powers of the presbytery are inherent, and the powers of the General Assembly are derived. Our church was organized from the bottom up, so the powers given to the General Assembly by the presbyteries were only those specifically named. Thus, in our parlance it is incorrect to speak of "Presbyterian Headquarters" as being in Louisville, Kentucky. If there is a "headquarters," it is the presbytery, or even the session of the particular church. In very real terms, the sessions in the Presbyterian system are where the basic decisions are made, and that is true now more than ever.

Although many writers make broad references to the many differences and serious disagreements in our church, the argument is also made that particular churches (local congregations) are more homogeneous than ever, by race, theological perspective, administrative style, mission emphases, and all the rest. The authors of *Vital Signs* unequivocally state two important things in successive sentences: "[R]eligious vitality exists in local congregations. Any rebuilding of ecosystems of nurture must therefore begin with a focus on congregations."[1] The issues in the local congregation that bind us together in understanding and in predilection are at least three: (a) congregations in the Presbyterian Church (U.S.A.) are alive and well; (b) a primary purpose for presbyteries is to support the particular church; and (c) there are healing and reforming steps that congregations can take to be faithful and effective in their witness and mission.

Congregations in the Presbyterian Church (U.S.A.) are alive and well

Few of us are likely to know much about the Presbyterian Church in Commerce, Georgia. But perhaps we should. As a part of their calling to be a church that nurtures members, every three months each member is given three names, and the member is requested to pray for those three persons during that quarter of the year. Three months later each member receives three more names. One Commerce member in her nineties lives in a retirement home. She cannot get to church, with the result that she knows fewer and fewer of the members of the congregation. So she telephones the three persons for whom she is to pray and asks each, "What would you like me to pray about?" In that way she gets to know newer and younger members. Who knows what ties bind together this congregation!

The same woman who makes the telephone calls, and who prays, lost a sister, but she could not attend the sister's memorial service. The young pastor knew of her situation, and he asked if she would like him to have a brief memorial service in her room. She would, and he did. Pastoral care is limited only by our time—and our creativity. It happens at the congregational level.

From Commerce, take a free flight from Hartsfield Airport in Atlanta to LAX in Los Angeles for a visit to the Presbyterian Church in Claremont, California. If we are fortunate, we may be present for the annual joyful, up-tempo beat of the jazz band in their jazz service. Everyone in the congregation claps and beats the pews in rhythm as the band, the choir, and all present lustily sing, "When the Saints Come Marching In." Anyone who has never sung "What a Friend We Have in Jesus" jazz-style has truly missed an opportunity to sing about prayer in a style of praise and thanksgiving that is unforgettable.

But, if one misses that jazz service, which has become a fixture after ten years, there is always the twentieth (in 1998) annual joint worship with the nearby Jewish temple, complete with cantor for music and the rabbi as preacher. And then the larger Anglo congregation joins annually with the Emmanuel Hispanic congregation for joint worship in two languages. For fifty-one Sundays they worship in the same sanctuary, but at different times. Anyone who thinks Reformed worship must be dull should buy her or his own ticket to fly to where worship is varied and alive, with children of all ages participating, and where biblical preaching is at the heart of the life of the church. There are continuing education events for all ages, a youth mission trip, and involvement in all kinds of local mission, plus strong support of the unified mission of presbytery, synod, and the General Assembly.

No ticket this time, but anyone can bum a ride to Bel Air Presbyterian Church, Los Angeles, which hosts every Sunday an evening worship service and discussion for college and university students. Normally about three hundred come from several area colleges. From there, we can go quickly by plane, or some six-plus hours by car, up the coastal highway or the valley of California to the Lafayette-Orinda Presbyterian Church. In addition to a full "regular" program, that church hosts about three hundred singles each Sunday evening from all over the Bay Area.

Some of us would resist going to the hub of Northwest Airlines in Minneapolis in the winter, en route to the nearby St. Luke's Presbyterian Church in Wayzata, Minnesota. To be a member in that inclusive fellowship, a person is strongly urged to participate on a regular basis in some local mission effort, for instance, relating to a Native American ministry, which sometimes means leaving home for a period on a work project; or joining with others in an affordable housing effort in the larger community; a food shelf program; or participating in an intergenerational activity. In many churches segregation by ages tends to prevent easy conversations and relationships with persons of various ages and perspectives. A conscious effort is made at St. Luke's to integrate younger and older persons in church programs of every kind; intentionality is the key.

The next stop might be the Spring Valley Presbyterian Church of Columbia, South Carolina. Some readers doubtless know about their specialty, when some 1,300 Presbyterian churches, in addition to 4,200 other churches, join with them in their specialty: a "Souper Bowl." Participating congregations ask their members to contribute $1.00 each on the Sunday in late January when the National Football League's Super Bowl is held. The total special offering is given to designated charities that feed the hungry. Advertising for this event is now given free at the Super Bowl. In 1997 over $1.5 million was donated through this program to different hunger programs. There is a special twist to this program. It began at Spring Valley in 1988 in response to the pastoral prayer of the pastor.

Even if any one particular church is not now a "Souper Bowl Church," we join in rejoicing at how other parts of this body are reaching out in some dimension of mission. Ninety percent of Presbyterian Church (U.S.A.) congregations now have *some* hunger program; we have united in at least initial efforts to conquer the evil that citizens, particularly children, go to bed hungry.

One more stop. The airport is named Bluegrass, and the city is Lexington, Kentucky. Second Presbyterian Church there has over 1,100 members, and it has something else: a parish nurse. A growing number of churches are reminding us of an earlier Presbyterian concern with health issues, except that the issue of ministering to the whole person is no longer about new Presbyterian hospitals for the sick, but about wellness programs for the well, or at least for persons who are not sick in bed. Local church health programs are perceived as justice issues, peace issues, issues related to the integrity of creation, and spiritual issues. It has long been recognized that illness has an impact not just upon an individual or upon just one family, but upon an entire congregation. At Second Church the parish nurse is a member of the healing team with a holistic approach to health. Beginning in 1990, the church added a parish nurse to its staff and opened its own health education center, offering blood pressure screenings; visits to the home, nursing home, and hospital; caregiver classes; assistance in referrals to various health and social service agencies; and individual teaching and counseling.[2]

No time machine is in operation to provide conclusive proof, but from all reported studies, in the early history of our country congregations were primarily concerned with their own survival and maintaining with integrity their own congregational worship and nurture. Only secondarily were they concerned with church planting, or what we frequently call church extension. Finding qualified preachers and leaders of worship in the colonies was an extremely arduous process when travel was so hazardous and all of the early preachers were émigrés from some other place, mostly the British Isles. New church development priorities came later. It is surely true that a key function of the first presbyteries was the recruiting, training, and ordaining of ministers. Much later, emphases upon corporate mission through the various governing bodies became prominent.

Throughout our entire history in this nation particular Presbyterian churches have had a vision to multiply through growth beyond the existing churches. For years the pattern was for the "First Church" in a given town or city to begin a mission, a Sunday school, or a preaching point with the clear intention of eventually organizing a new congregation which would itself become self-supporting. Presbyteries were more seriously expected to perform that function in some parts of the country than others. One is in awe with the realization of how many new churches were begun from the First Presbyterian Church of Seattle, or Baltimore, or Nashville, or many other large cities, or even in smaller cities such as Berkeley, California.

It is also a matter of record that many particular congregations began work that seemed a meager response, at first, to massive social problems, but which blossomed into major efforts with widespread support, in efforts to meet chronic problems of poverty, sweatshops for children, inadequate and substandard housing, and racial discrimination. It seems, however, that the majority of Presbyterian congregations in the nineteenth century increasingly saw their role as supporting financially the mission work that others were doing on their behalf—especially, of course, in foreign countries.

For many years congregations in the Presbyterian Church in the United States participated in local mission, or through their presbytery Home Mission Committee. The focus of mission at the congregational level did not return in theory or in practice, generally, in the United Presbyterian Church in the U.S.A. until the adoption in 1969 of what was tagged "Overture H." Much of the thrust of the overture, which became ecclesiastical law, was related to denominational structure, but at its heart, also, was the principle that mission should take place at the level of the lowest governing body that could administer and support it. Both "administer" and "support" are important words. Particularly in the UPCUSA, which differed somewhat, as we have noted, from the Presbyterian Church in the United States, a great part of the mission effort had been defined and supported at the national level. The new effort at determining mission by congregations through their sessions was a radical departure from previous procedures. The decline in giving to General Assembly mission was both a cause and a result of the change in the administration of mission. The change of location for the administration of some forms of mission, in turn, led to a further decrease in mission giving at the denominational level. So, it was both/and.

This historic agreed-upon change of location in emphasis for some kinds of mission was not without its problems, though. "The congregation is now the locus of power and mission in American Presbyterianism. But congregations are also characterized by tremendous diversity and frequently by confusion about their own identities."[3]

A primary purpose for presbyteries is to support particular churches

Indeed, the formation of presbyteries in the Middle Colonies came about because congregations recognized that they needed assistance in recruiting and training, and in ordering the status and functions of ministers. The location and availability of possible pastors for congregations might not be known to any one congregation in its isolation. And, of course, standards for ordination had to be adopted when it became apparent that there would never be a sufficient number of pastors coming from across the ocean.

In 1990, two astute observers of the Presbyterian scene wrote about the dichotomy between what they called the governing body church and the congregational church, and there is surely truth in their distinction.[4] At their best through the years, however, presbyteries in particular, as well as the General Assembly, have sought to provide resources for congregations in all kinds of ways. Some congregations have complained that neither their presbytery nor their synod, nor the General Assembly, has been sufficiently attentive to their needs. On the other hand, some presbyteries, a few synods, a number of offices at the General Assembly level, and even some seminaries have tried to offer assistance in a variety of ways, but they complain that pastors and elders refused to avail themselves of opportunities offered. Again, truth surely abounds.

A recurring question arises: What are presbyteries doing to highlight outstanding mission ventures in particular churches? Creative and innovative programming needs to be shared, and most presbyteries have newsletters of various kinds, but purposefully sharing the endeavors in a congregation can reinforce and encourage the good work being done in a particular church. There is also value in alerting all the churches to an approach, or in sharing new information about resources for replicating in other places what is working well in one place. Nearby churches can be invited to join in a broader-based ministry with and for high school students from different congregations who may attend the same school. Single-congregation youth groups need not feel small and isolated, and in typical Presbyterian openness some of the youth groups united in a common mission may not need to be Presbyterian. Aware and awake presbytery committees can provide linkages which may not be visible to just one congregation.

Not surprisingly, we turn to the *Book of Order*, looking first at chapter IX on "Governing Bodies," especially reviewing section 4, "Principles of Administration." There we note, in the provisions for review of the next lower governing body, that the review of a session by a presbytery is for the purpose of helping the session, and thereby, of course, the entire congregation.[5] The review is not held in order to find a reason to discipline the session, or to find fault with it. The presbytery, as a presbytery, does not benefit from the review of the work of sessions, although the presbytery has an interest in seeing that all sessions within its bounds act "decently and in order." Beyond that, the entire purpose of the review is to be helpful. In chapter XI of the *Book of Order*, in section 11, there are listed twenty-seven duties and responsibilities of a presbytery.[6] Of these twenty-seven, twelve relate directly to ways in which the presbytery is to help the session or congregation, and a number of other duties are concerned with the matter of pastors of churches and candidates for the ministry. Legalities aside, the true issue is whether or not the presbytery genuinely desires to provide resources, assistance, and support of many kinds to the churches.

Every Sunday morning in San Gabriel Presbytery, worship

is conducted in ten—that's right, ten—different languages; in New York City the number is nine! Instead of being divisive for a presbytery with multiple language and cultural groups, the corporate church can share whatever wisdom and experience it has garnered from other ethnic-oriented congregations that may have been struggling with some of the same kinds of problems and opportunities.

Many, if not most, presbyteries, similarly, are ready and able to provide assistance in each of the nineteen areas of responsibilities that sessions have, which are listed in chapter X of the *Book of Order*.[7]

With governing bodies and congregations looking to each other, and when we all know and believe in the system, why do troubles develop? In our experience in the Presbyterian Church, those sessions, presbyteries, synods, and the General Assembly, and the staffs in each case, including pastors, work best together who quite intentionally turn to each other for support, wisdom, learning, and, when necessary, help. The converse is also true, in our experience. If a session is not in the habit of having one or more of its members as regular participants in all phases of the life of the presbytery, that session is the one most disenchanted with Presbyterian policy and procedure, and the members of those sessions are lost when faced with a pastoral problem, for instance. The General Assembly, synod, or presbytery official or member who has little respect for or desire to work with congregations—perhaps because there is not full agreement all along the line, or there is some personality conflict—is a potential source of trouble, waiting to erupt.

It is also our experience that those elders and ministers who know and love the *Book of Order*, and who are committed to the Presbyterian system of process and procedures, are rarely the ones who become unhappy at one thing or another, or with many things. Trying to know the people and learning how things work in good times serves doubly well in times of crisis, tension, or confusion. Further, we have learned that a little humility and some old-fashioned caring and grace go a long way. The ability to listen should be a growth industry for us all. Rodney King's question, "Can't we all just get along?" has come as a plea from one man terrorized by police in Los Angeles. But that plaint is one which might well be on the lips of all of us who honestly try to be faithful to Christ and to one another. We give credence to an old aphorism: If it doesn't happen in the local church, it doesn't happen.

There are healing and reforming steps that congregations can take to be faithful and effective in their witness and mission

In our experience and observation alive congregations exhibit one or more characteristics that struggling churches might emulate.

1. The revival of the teaching role of the pastor. Nearly all Presbyterians give lip service, at least, to the desirability of restoring a function that has been lost in many places: encouraging the pastor to reassume the art of being the teaching elder. The Bible needs to be taught, and the preacher needs to be a teaching preacher, in addition to whatever other teaching responsibilities the pastor has during the week. Pastoral care, administration, and such things as counseling are all important, but revival of the congregation is likely to begin in a teaching pulpit. Many commentators have noted what we have observed: In many congregations the pastor's "study" has become the pastor's "office," and the latter designation is revealing; it may indicate the perceived lack of depth in pastoral study, and, therefore, of a less effective teaching ministry.

2. A vital and alive organization of Presbyterian Women is nearly always a sign of a reforming church. It is our conviction that consistently through the years the place where the total program of the Presbyterian Church has received publicity, informed interpretation, and ready and willing support through interested and caring people has been through the Women of the Church in the former Presbyterian Church in the United States, United Presbyterian Women in the United

Presbyterian Church U.S.A., and Presbyterian Women in the Presbyterian Church (U.S.A.). Presbytery meetings rarely provide a full and balanced understanding of the church program, but meetings of the women of the presbytery do. Triennial National Gatherings of Presbyterian Women are biblical, inspirational, and programmatically sound, with a wide variety of meaningful course offerings. Wise pastors, whether female or male, support Presbyterian Women and keep abreast of what is happening in that usually very dedicated group. Better interpretation of the mission of the church does not happen anywhere else within the system, including the display areas at the annual General Assembly, in our judgment. No other group supports mission financially so well as Presbyterian Women routinely do. This is not a paid commercial!

3. Studies indicate that 59 percent of the members of Presbyterian churches were reared in other churches. If this is so, and we have no reason to doubt it, new member classes and officer training courses need to receive major attention in *every* particular church.[8] The Presbyterian ethos must be taught unapologetically, as well as Reformed theology, Presbyterian polity, a basic understanding of why we do what we do in worship, and what we are about in mission, locally and around the world. Is it too much to say that throughout the total education program of our churches—for children, youth, and adults—that we should stress our Reformed heritage, our memories, and our traditions?

4. One prescription for revitalizing congregations is very difficult: invite people to church. There is not a Presbyterian in America who does not agree that we should all invite people to church, but it is no joke that this simple matter is very difficult to do—for many of us. We simply are very uncomfortable inviting people to church, or, maybe, we just think it *would* be uncomfortable if we ever did it! Whatever the reality, we are united in the conviction that we should invite all kinds of people to come to church with us (coming *with* us can often be a key), but if we truly want a reforming congregation, we need to put our best intentions into practice.

5. Alive congregations do everything possible to make the church look and feel like home. Somewhere in one of his books Lyle Schaller says that the way you can tell a caring church is to check on two things: its outside bulletin board and its rest rooms (presumably the inside ones). His point is obvious. If those two things are clean, neat, and kept current, other things will be, too, you can surmise. Thus, those of us who truly love our worship and education facilities, and want to share them with others, will take care of them. Little things also say, "Welcome!" or, "We don't care."

6. "If Presbyterians are serious about revitalization, they need to say something about sacred time and how it should be used, something about the disciplines of personal life, and something about how these matters should figure in the life of the church."[9] The author of these words was writing about Sabbath observance, really the absence, now, of such observance. His contention is that formerly, by making a special day of Sunday—when we did not work, nor attend movies, nor do lots of other things, but instead emphasized what he calls "the disciplines of personal life,"—we understood much better the meaning of worship, and that "the erosion of Sabbath observance" is really the "erosion of faith in general."[10] If there is time that we should set aside for the nurture of our faith, does not that mean, in part at least, that each Christian, maybe even especially adults, should engage in regular systematic study—of the Bible or of Christian ethics, church history, or whatever helps us grow in faith and in knowledge? What portion of Sunday do we regularly preserve for nurturing our faith and deepening our relationship with God and with Christ's church? When do we read books that enrich our spiritual development or confront us with consequential ethical and moral matters?

7. The church must do both evangelism and social action. Leonard Sweet has written:

> The primary function of the church is not to be an intellectual or missionary movement. The primary function of the church is not to be a political or social justice movement.

The primary purpose of the church is not to change the world, or to preach to the world, or to serve the world. The primary function of the church, from which stem all the other functions, is to *be* the body of Christ—quite sacramentally, Christ enfleshed, incarnated, embodied in presence and in power."[11]

Grayson Tucker has countered with this statement:

The church's inner life stands on an equal footing with its two thrusts outward, evangelization and social action. The mission of the church is not simply evangelism plus social involvement; the church's mission is these two plus the "strong heart," a vibrant internal life.[12]

Here Tucker quotes the words of Sweet, given above, and goes on to add the note which Presbyterians have also endorsed:

The metaphor of a two-armed church with a strong heart mandates that "the primary function" in this quote be changed to read "an essential dimension of the mission." Any effort to lift up one of these three aspects over the others leads to distortion.[13]

Presbyterians have historically taught this principle of *being* the body of Christ, but the caveat attached is also most appropriate. This is to say that the church must *be* the body of Christ, and it must emphasize the key functions of evangelism with integrity, and social action with compassion. These are bedrock convictions of the Reformed tradition.

8. "The health of a congregation is directly related to its sense of mission."[14] This basic tenet is related to the whole issue of relating mission action to membership growth. Few converts to Christianity are made or members added to a church roll as a result of social justice or human rights issues that target them as potential converts, but people are attracted to the church, often to become a permanent part of its constituency, *because of* the mission outreach which nonmembers observe and support, and thereby they become members. The definition and fulfillment of mission in and of itself gives health to a particular church. The old adage is that a church which gives to mission also gives to its own support. An entire membership, including all of its leadership, can become converted to a new level of commitment and a new depth of grace and growth through mission involvement.

9. Conflict within a church does not mean an ill congregation. "How to fight fairly in marriage" is a hot topic for premarital counseling or newlyweds, or for those celebrating twenty-five years together. The issue is not disagreement, but how disagreement is handled.

Amateur foreign policy strategists wonder why politicians are prone to break off diplomatic relations when that act closes the possibility of further conversations. So it is in married life, or within a church community. One valid purpose of some discussions is just to "keep talking," hoping, praying, and believing that through God's Spirit a deepened and enriched understanding and appreciation of the other side's position might yet provide the means of a new level of proposals and counterproposals to work through the seemingly insoluble problem.

To put it in affirmative terms: Whenever we find a church that can debate openly, fairly, and without rancor or personal attacks, we know that there is love, respect, and always the possibility— or likelihood—of resolution. To make it unmistakably clear, an open and tolerant attitude in a church can be a healthy church that is in the process of becoming revitalized. While to outsiders, any open disagreement may seem to be irreconcilable discord, the reality can be a very healthy church, indeed.

10. A revitalized church is a vibrant part of the denomination. That may seem self-serving, but it is valid, we believe. There is strength in numbers, of course, but we Presbyterians take our fellowship very seriously. Long before the World Council of Churches was organized in 1948, the World Alliance of Reformed Churches was organized in 1875. We rejoice in our heritage and in our interaction with each other, both within the Presbyterian Church (U.S.A.), in the World

Alliance, and in the National and World Councils of Churches. Congregations on the sidelines of the life of their presbyteries isolate themselves from one source of stimulation and possible renewal. It is not quite the same context, but John Mackay, when president of Princeton Seminary, would talk about people who have a balcony view of religion— looking on from outside (or above) the encounter.

11. The re-forming church reviews its duties and responsibilities as defined in the *Book of Order*, including the Directory for Worship.[15] This task can be viewed as a chore, but it can also be a time of learning, reflection, and great satisfaction to review and contemplate what the future might hold as these principles and guidelines are carefully read and discussed.

We are wonderfully united in that hundreds of congregations have found life and vitality following these principles. They have changed lives over and over again. We praise God when we hear people say, "God called me through my church. I had no choice but to respond."

> I love Thy kingdom, Lord,
> The house of Thine abode,
> The church our blest Redeemer saved
> With His own precious blood.
>
> I love Thy church, O God;
> Her walls before Thee stand,
> Dear as the apple of Thine eye,
> And graven on Thy hand.
>
> For her my tears shall fall,
> For her my prayers ascend;
> To her my cares and toils be given,
> Till toils and cares shall end.
>
> Beyond my highest joy
> I prize her heavenly ways,
> Her sweet communion, solemn vows,
> Her hymns of love and praise.

Sure as Thy truth shall last,
To Zion shall be given
The brightest glories earth can yield,
And brighter bliss of heaven.
            (Timothy Dwight)[16]

11

Presbyterians Do It
Decently and in Order

Our Polity

The old gospel hymn "Standing on the Promises" had a swinging tune that was quite singable, and the chorus had a firm ending phrase, "Standing on the promises of God." The promises were never quite spelled out in the hymn, but that was all right because singers understood that the "promises of God" were related to God's promises to Israel and to redemption for those elected by God as people came to receive forgiveness for sin and the grace and love of God in Jesus Christ. Anyone who has lived through a major flood, either the slow-moving kind or the flash flood variety, knows the horror of weak and sinking foundations. Get ready for a shock!

The polity of the Reformed tradition is built on sin. And that *is* true, at least in part. Let us review a bit.

There are three basic forms of church government: (a) *episcopal*, in which the bishop is an authority—examples are the Roman Catholic Church, the Episcopal Church, and the United Methodist Church; (b) *congregational*, where the local congregation exercises the predominant power and authority; examples are the Baptists, the Congregationalists, and the United Church of Christ, though the last named church has a modified version; and (c) *presbyterian* government, in which rule is by elders. Our form comes between the other two, with not just one person fully in charge, nor all members. In our system, the presbytery is the collective bishop which makes the decisions in ordaining ministers, approving the calls to pastors, dissolving pastoral relationships, organizing churches, dissolving or merging churches, providing care and oversight of congregations, providing oversight for and preparing persons for the ministry as candidates, sending commissioners—and overtures—to higher governing bodies, receiving and voting upon proposed amendments, hearing appeals and resolving conflicts, and so forth.

Rule by Elders

Why was our form of government chosen? Because of sin. Remember who were the arbitrary despots at the time of the Reformation. They were the rulers of the principalities, and, of course, the ecclesiastical bishops, the cardinals, and the pope. And they were the perceived sinners who were not to be trusted—ergo, a collective bishop is brought onto the scene, a committee, to make all the decisions. No one was fooled, of course, as all knew that a group of people can be a collective sinner, but it was felt that a group was much less likely to be arrogant and arbitrary than just one person, acting often in that person's own best interests.

There was more to it than that, of course, and we return to the major Reformed emphasis on the "priesthood of all believers" principle. No one person was to be the sole ruler, bishop, or whatever, as the functions of priest and prophet were also dispersed among many. One imagines that the Reformers must have read what Samuel, the last of the judges of Israel, had to say when the people wanted a king so they could "be like other people." Samuel predicted accurately what would happen: The kings would make vassals of the people, call them to serve in his army, accumulate personal wealth, and all the other anticipated evils. Thus, one of the principles of Presbyterian government, or polity, is a collective rule and joint decision-making to reduce the potential sin of despotism. The process of making decisions by committee is cumbersome, slow, and probably inefficient much of the time, but it has decided advantages.

It is worth noting in this connection that a church pastor can do very little alone. Some sessions have been known to allow a pastor to become a tyrant or dictator, but they are very naughty and negligent (as is the presbytery) to allow anything like that to happen. The pastor alone can baptize no one; can make no decision about the use of the church property, or about who can become a member or cease to be a member; cannot fire the organist or employ a secretary. Although the pastor is the moderator of the session that has the power to make decisions in these things, and has authority to speak— and to exercise great leadership, to be sure—the pastor can do none of these things without an action of the session. The pastor can choose the hymns and the scripture for the sermon— and preach!

In our era, particularly, when everyone wants "a piece of the action," we are fortunate in having a tested and finely honed and experienced means of conducting our business with all kinds of perspectives, insights, and worldviews brought to bear by ethnic minorities, women, the physically challenged, and the chronologically gifted on the multitude of subjects which confront any group in our culture.

1. The Church Is Community

At first blush we might tend to think that congregational polity has a better understanding of community than representative government has. But remember: The session is community, as are the congregation, presbytery, synod, and the General Assembly when we fully grasp that we are a connectional church, and that the communal nature of the church is inclusive—of all tongues and nationalities, races, both sexes, the physically challenged, the chronologically gifted, the mentally special—inclusive of the universal visible church and of the invisible church. The invisible church includes "all the saints who from their labors rest." Pope John XXIII is one of us! Who would not love the opportunity to confer with John Huss; or to ask Barnabas how he felt when Paul left him because he, Barnabas, wanted to take the young John Mark with him; or to ask the first missionary of the modern era, William Carey, about his challenging sermon, "Expect Great Things from God; Attempt Great Things for God!" before he sailed for India.

We do not often think of how our polity reflects community. The theory of doing things decently and in order is, in part, to act as Christian ladies and gentlemen with each other as we seek to find the will of God in orderly and temperate debate. A "pro" speaker is followed, in turn, by a "con" speaker. We do not leap down each other's throats, but each time we speak it is to and through a neutral moderator whose role is to be impartial and fair. If we undertake to discuss "decently," we do not accuse each other of having no faith, or of spreading lies, and what we write for our sermons and in our books and periodicals is, to the best of our ability and knowledge, accurate and balanced, as we give the other person, and any other position, the benefit of the doubt.

At the close of the meeting of whatever kind, how wonderful to overhear disinterested observers comment, "How those Christians love one another!" That is the goal for which we strive, and it is the basis for our form of government. "We are not divided; all one body, we" is our marching orders, not off to war, but off to seek reconciliation, harmony, and common ground. "Decently and in order" does not come easily for people who fully realize and accept that their relationship is also based on sin, but who strive to be a covenant community, based on a God of forgiving grace and steadfast love, who showed so clearly that God was willing to become human with us, and to face our temptations, our problems, and to walk with us as we yearn to "walk humbly with our God."

But we are fortunate in far more ways than that. No one person in a Presbyterian Church is alone; we are in community, in the Old Testament called a covenant community or fellowship. God made a covenant with various of the chosen leaders of Israel, but the covenant was always with them as representatives of the people of God, the covenant community, and the covenant is ever-renewing as God relates to the continuing descendants of the evolving community of faith. God has always chosen leaders to have special functions and responsibilities, but they have served as representatives of the covenant community, with whom God's everlasting contract is made.

Government by elders was related to the manner in which Jethro urged Moses to appoint elders to aid in "church administration," pastoral care and discipline of the community. Government by elders is also, of course, a New Testament term that referred to the chosen leaders of the early Christian communities. Government by elders was also related to politics in Geneva, Switzerland, under John Calvin. Calvin was thoroughly familiar with what little is said in the New Testament about church government. Bishops, elders, and deacons are all mentioned, but their specific duties and obligations are not clear, though the function of the deacons is most obvious in their call to a ministry of service. Presbyter is the Greek word for "elder," and for Presbyterians "elders" has meant those persons elected by congregations to provide leadership in the particular church as members of the session, often called "ruling elders." A second kind of elder familiar to generations of Presbyterians has been the "teaching elder," a term traditionally used for ministers, although teaching is often not regarded as a chief function of every minister these days. The elders, when serving together, are the governing body for the local group of gathered Christians. Both kinds of elders often serve very effectively together in higher governing bodies.

2. The Special Bond of Ordination

A further important indication of our mutual relationship is known by ordained persons, but not always immediately called to mind. Ordination is not only for life, but ordination is to and for the whole church. If a person ordained in Little Rock receives a call to a faculty position at Mary Baldwin College in Staunton, Virginia, she need not be ordained a second time if elected an elder in her new home church. Similarly, a minister ordained in Omaha who is called to a pastorate in Syracuse can be installed without having a second ordination.

Representative Government

We do not have a pure democracy, but a representative form of government, quite similar to the civil system in the United States. Instead of city council, county, state, and federal government, we have session, presbytery, synod, and General Assembly. Every governing body, sometimes called a court, sometimes called a judicatory, above the session has an equal number of "ruling" elders and "teaching" elders, or ministers of word and sacrament. We call it *parity*. All sessions have far more elected elders than ministers, but in other governing bodies the number of elders and ministers is identical, and there are certain provisions that make that policy operable in all kinds of situations. The Reformers rejected sacerdotalism, the name given to rule by priests, or generally, the paid professionals. All church members are "represented" by those relatively few who are elected to be the elders for that congregation.

1. Presbyters do not seek the will of the people, but the will of Christ

This is a fundamental principle that holds us together, not always well understood. Persons elected for leadership responsibilities do represent, that is, come from, the body that elects them, but they are not to take a poll of that body to see how the representatives should vote. Rather, this representative should seek the will of God in concert with all other elders in a session, and with all presbyters in a meeting of a higher governing body. This is part of the covenant between God and the people. God's will is to be done, insofar as any human group can ascertain God's plan, and we all know that we horribly fail. The grace and mercy come in the fact that we are always seeking to reform just because we know that we are sinners, and our polity is built upon sin—in part!

An illustration is that there are no proxy votes in Presbyterian governing bodies. Why? For the fundamental theological reason that when a governing body assembles, it is assumed that that body will seek the will of God. If a person had cast her or his ballot ahead of time, that person could not have been present to adjust or amend a decision, if deemed necessary, from what she or he had previously decided and written down, without hearing the Spirit of God speak in a corporate setting—session, presbytery, synod, or General Assembly. Perhaps through the insights and language of someone whose experiences and outlooks are not nearly the same, an absent person's decision might have been drastically changed had she or he been present for the discussion before the vote was taken. The absent person fails to hear people speak about reasons or sensitivities that she or he may never have had occasion to consider.

Counting votes can never be done ahead of time, since people may not vote even approximately as they had planned or as they had told others they expected to vote. Yes, it can be risky to listen to the voice of God. God might want us to cross the Red Sea when an enemy army is pursuing us from behind, or to cross the Jordan River in faith to a land occupied by defenders who are not eager to be moved. Proxy voting is not permitted, and the hope and expectation is that everyone present will be listening to the pros and cons in a debate as each person seeks to ascertain the will of God and articulate the person's insights and convictions for that assembled community at that time.

God rules and overrules, or in Calvin's great conviction, God is sovereign. This is further reason why we must try to take very seriously our understanding of the work of the Holy Spirit. God's Spirit might move us collectively in ways that individually we might never have thought possible. Isaiah spoke for too few of us in Isaiah 6:5: "Woe is me! I am lost, for I am a man of unclean lips, and I live among a people of unclean lips." Not many of us confess that we are part of a sinful community with an inadequate comprehension of what God is saying to us corporately. If the unison Prayer of Confession in a worship service does not fully give voice to our feelings, we can speak our own privately and then later share our thoughts with worship leaders for possible future use.

A common distraught cry from many members upon hearing of an action by a Presbyterian governing body is, "They surely don't speak for me." Right! It is not intended that an elder or a minister commissioner should cast a vote in the precise manner in which a majority of a session or a congregation might have previously thought wisest. The governing body purports to speak *to* me from the leading of God's Spirit, and not *for* me. Until and unless church members comprehend this principle in depth, they may never be comfortable in the Presbyterian Church and its understanding of representative polity, or governance. A popular referendum will never be tried in the Presbyterian Church because the church is not seeking a popular vote or a poll on any issue; the church corporately seeks to ascertain the will of God, and that is often a great deal tougher to do than to just pull together a bunch of individual votes or to make a series of judgments.

Few presbyters could attest that their potential vote had never been changed after listening to thoughtful debates or discussions. Our church provides a magnificent experience for those commissioners to the General Assembly who have the unforgettable experience of sitting next to an alert, thoughtful, prepared, and committed Youth Advisory Delegate. The variety of perspectives and viewpoints can be mind-blowing, particularly as most of us have a penchant for normally conferring with people who are most like us—and most Presbyterians who vote in governing bodies are no longer young.

2. The session is responsible to the presbytery

There is rarely a church officer training event wherein many, if not a majority, state that the session is responsible to the congregation that elected the elders. Wrong! The key to grasping this concept is found in the word "review." A presbytery is to "review session minutes and records at least once each year."[1] That means a presbytery can make all kinds of suggestions for the good of the session as it reviews the session's work annually. Important operative language for a presbytery here is: "to coordinate the work of its member churches";[2] "to counsel with a particular church";[3] "to provide encouragement, guidance, and resources to its member churches in the areas of leadership development, church officer training, worship, nurture, witness, service, stewardship, equitable compensation, personnel policies, and fair employment practices";[4] and "to provide pastoral care for the churches . . . , visiting sessions and ministers on a regular basis."[5] Thus the session is responsible for the faithful performance of its duties to the presbytery, although it has every reason, of course, to share with its own congregation what decisions have been reached, and to give the reasons for some of those actions.

How dare they, we say. Think a moment about the judicial system operative in the United States. Ultimately, the Supreme Court has the right to reverse or to let stand a decision of the lower courts. A presbytery's primary function, however, is not to judge what a session has done, but to counsel with the session when there is trouble, to suggest possible ways and methods of procedure, to commend what is going well, to encourage, and to provide the particular church with resources and helps of all kinds.

Nearly all persons in church officer training for the first time come to recognize that they had failed to realize the means by which a presbytery reviews the session. Primarily, the review is done through the presbytery's careful and thoughtful annual reading of the minutes of each session within its bounds. One key measure of the adequacy and helpfulness of a presbytery is the carefulness with which the presbytery, usually through one of its committees, reads the minutes of the sessions that comprise that presbytery. Some presbyteries have an established process by which the committee that is responsible for reading session minutes highlights and shares with the presbytery some of the creative and innovative actions that sessions are taking so that other sessions, too, might consider undertaking the same kinds of significant things.

Like review, jurisdiction is by the higher governing body, and it is a shared responsibility. There is no Presbyterian "bishop" to make decisions because the governing body is a collective bishop. Those who transfer into the Presbyterian Church from churches with an episcopal form of church government might do well to consider what powers, duties, and responsibilities the bishop has, and then comprehend that the care and oversight functions belong to the presbytery, not to just one person.

Christ called the church into being

It seems to us that something else needs to be said in this chapter, whether it is called a Prologue or a Summation. We can open the subject by asking a question: Why this Presbyterian order? or Why does structure matter? In the Reformed tradition the response is profound. The first chapter in the *Book of Order* is clear: Christ called the church into being.[6] Surely the church of Jesus Christ is to be ultimately in every country, and that means that the church will be both inclusive and diverse.

Only the Roman Catholic Church has sought to justify its form of government, or church polity, with such thoughtfulness and intentionality as has the Reformed or Presbyterian Church. John Calvin was convinced that a church lives out its theology in the way it conducts its business.[7] Decisions are not made in an autocratic manner, as we have stressed; the desire of the group is determined by majority vote—after the will of God has been conscientiously sought through prayer and discussion, led by the Holy Spirit. Governing bodies do not always get it right, for "all synods and councils may err."[8]

The individual Christian is not only redeemed in Jesus Christ; each person is called into service, and there must be as many ways to serve as there are people elected in the fellowship of the church to broad, diversified, and continuing opportunities for service. David Little has used a beautiful and felicitous phrase: "The Christian is elected or called to order." There we have it: The Christian is called to order. "He [sic] who is elected in Christ finds his personhood by taking his place in the harmonious structure of the holy community."[9]

Theology and polity are intertwined. The very integrity of the body can be maintained or lost by the way the governing body conducts its business. For good reason Calvin thought long and hard about polity in the Reformed church, and we are his ecclesiastical heirs. We joke a great deal about our multitude of committee, session, presbytery, synod, and General Assembly meetings, and we need to take much of it in a light vein, but we also need to remember that we are constantly working on our continuing effort to reform this great church whose very method of procedure, whose very processes, bind us together in a community of believers who trust one another in process. Each has a fair opportunity—both to seek to ascertain God's will, and to try to do what we believe is God's guidance.

> A mighty fortress is our God,
> A bulwark never failing;
> Our helper He amid the flood
> Of mortal ills prevailing.
> For still our ancient foe
> Doth seek to work us woe;
> His craft and power are great,
> And armed with cruel hate,
> On earth is not his equal.
>
> Did we in our own strength confide,
> Our striving would be losing;
> Were not the right Man on our side,
> The Man of God's own choosing.
> Dost ask who that may be?
> Christ Jesus, it is He,
> Lord Sabaoth His name,
> From age to age the same,
> And He must win the battle.
>
> And though this world, with devils filled,
> Should threaten to undo us,
> We will not fear, for God hath willed

His truth to triumph through us.
The prince of darkness grim,
We tremble not for him;
His rage we can endure,
For lo! his doom is sure,
One little word shall fell him.

That word above all earthly powers,
No thanks to them, abideth;
The Spirit and the gifts are ours
Through Him who with us sideth;
Let goods and kindred go,
This mortal life also;
The body they may kill,
God's truth abideth still,
His kingdom is forever.

(Martin Luther)[10]

12

It's More Than a Grab Bag
Our Vast Array of Realities of Unity

Have you ever bought a vacuum cleaner, a "good buy," you thought, and then you took it home, opened the box—and made a discovery. You had not known that the purchase price included a clever attachment to make it easier to get dirt wedged in difficult-to-reach corners. Not only did you not get cheated, you had a greater bargain than you had expected! There may be a bushel of surprises like that in our Presbyterian community, some well known, but others a rare and marvelous bonus, called grace.

The Board of Pensions

From time to time when things were rough, many of us heard someone make the crack: "The only thing that holds this church together is the Pension Plan." In a very real sense the only reason for there to be a Presbyterian Board of Pensions is its communal nature. Secular companies could provide pensions and medical coverage for ministers and other church employees. Our Board practices the biblical ethic of sharing and caring for persons, based on need and the ability of Plan members to provide for themselves. The beauty of the Pension Plan, and its reason for being, is that those who have earned more share with those who have earned less.

It is truly a bond that unites. The funding for pensions is based on individual earnings, that is, the ability to pay into the Plan. And the benefits are for all members, proportionately more for members who have a lower income than they "earned." The median income of pastors is the floor so that, upon retirement, a person with a lifetime lower income is not penalized; the community of the Presbyterian family supplements what a person in a smaller church, usually, might otherwise receive. And, of course, there is no discrimination; men and women, older and younger persons, regardless of race or national origin—all pay the same percentage of income. Experience apportionments, a tremendous help against inflation, are given to both active and retired members of the Plan. Everyone shares. Plan members are truly bound together as equal sisters and brothers in Christ!

In a recent year the assets of the Board of Pensions were four billion dollars; some 60,000 persons, including dependents, are involved one way or another in the Pension Plan. The reason that health benefits can be less expensive than they otherwise would be is a feature that is true for other such groups, as well: Those who have fewer health problems help subsidize the highest costs of those who most need special care. It is all right to have warm fuzzy feelings in such circumstances for these cooperative endeavors and benefits. There was a time when opponents of a pension program for ministers felt such a thing showed a lack of faith.

PresbyTel

"Presby-who?" is not a question heard so frequently anymore since many have had occasion to call 1-800-UP-2-DATE (1-800-872-3283), but it is still called "the best-kept secret in the church." In 1996 PresbyTel handled 32,304 calls and presumably helped, gave answers to, or referred callers to the correct place for a response in most cases. Some 10,000 calls were handled during the one week of the General Assembly alone. That week it was open for business from 9:00 A.M. to 9:00 P.M. EDT. There is an overnight recording service, of course, so late-night calls can be dealt with the next morning.

This is known as helping each other, and the people who take all of those calls are so gracious that people have been known to say, "It makes you feel proud to be a Presbyterian." Calls come from every state, of course, and from Puerto Rico, as well as from Canada, England, Scotland, France, South

Africa, New Zealand, and Australia, to name a few, since the service is on the Internet. Responses can cover almost anything: Presbyterian News Service articles (1987 to the present); interpretations by the Advisory Committee on Social Witness Policy (from 1946); theological statements (1935–1989, soon to be updated); a listing of resources available through the Presbyterian Distribution Service; and recorded Minutes for Mission, book reviews, and the like on Voiceline, PresbyTel's audio information service (reached at the same number).

We are in this one together. PresbyTel is a wonderful service for all of us.

PresbyNet

This computer service for the Presbyterian family had some 5,000 members at the end of 1996, but nobody can count the vast number of messages that were transferred between and among individuals and groups called "meetings," some of them both innovative and extremely important. The Presbytery of Sierra Blanca in New Mexico, for instance, has helped every church in the presbytery to obtain a computer, subsidizing the hardware cost for smaller congregations, so everyone can keep in touch via PresbyNet, despite vast distances between churches. Stated Clerk Jim Rucker has remarked, "The electronic network does two things. It gives us a way to provide resources and communications directly to churches, and it draws us across distances into better community."[1] Other presbyteries with similar programs are Baltimore, Glacier, Missouri Union, and Yellowstone.

One other "all one big family, we" feeling is conveyed over PresbyNet because an increasing number of people are using this new tool to express appreciation to a person whose name is listed that day in the *Mission Yearbook for Prayer and Study*. A kind word for pastors and others can be readily sent through this medium. PresbyNet is less expensive than using a fax, and the services available continue to expand. "PresbyNews" is available each time it comes out, quicker, by far, than through the mail. Ecunet is a group similar to PresbyNet with fifteen ecumenical partners—so a user can connect with the Lutheran pastor in Chicago she or he may know; there is a "Prayer Chapel," and more. PresbyNet offers an Internet access program designed especially for Presbyterians. This is another service that keeps us in touch with each other, and theological discussions take place regularly. A Presbyterian World Wide Web site has been established (http://www.pcusa.org) with an increasing number of congregations—now over 1,000—presbyteries, synods, seminaries, campus ministries, and other organizations included. PresbyNet has arranged this connection with the Internet through UniDial, which provides 24-hour service support. The fee varies with the kind of access desired. It is anticipated that summer travelers will locate a church to visit through this new means.

Futurist Technology

Not everyone knows that Disney has under construction a high-tech planned development called Celebration Community, but they surely do know it in Central Florida Presbytery in their new church development on the site—Community Presbyterian Church in Celebration. The church construction progresses on its property on the Celebration grounds, which are like a traditional, small 1940s American downtown. But the reason for inclusion in this paragraph is that this church wants to model church programming technologically for the twenty-first century. The Welcome Center is to have information available about Presbyterian local, national, and worldwide mission. Sermons as well as pastoral letters are to go into parishioners' homes via Celebration's intranet. Small-group Bible studies are to take place by computer, as well as in group settings; elders fanned out for home communion will be plugged into simultaneous communion in the church sanctuary. The church has a home page on the community's intranet.[2] No one knows what will be next.

This kind of use of new technology can be a model of what can work and what doesn't work in using new methods, but also this project will be suggesting what is appropriate and what is not appropriate in this situation. The larger issue is whether many of us will feel wedded to older styles and more traditional methods, and thus be unwilling or unable to consider sharing in what others are learning. We can be united, at least, in one respect: We can all pray that the genuine gospel will be presented faithfully with integrity, knowing that some of our mission dollars are helping in new approaches that could possibly reach folks in a way our older ways of doing things may not, when some churches in some places do not find traditional methods helpful or appropriate any longer.

What does all this have to do with the rest of us? Well, the General Assembly in 1996 had special prayer for the development of this new congregation in Central Florida Presbytery, but read on.

The Presbyterian Investment and Loan Program (PILP)

We caught on quickly to the relationship. Right, a loan has been made to Community Church in Celebration. And why is that so good? PILP lends money for capital purposes to congregations, whether it be a new church development, church renovation, or a new education unit, for instance, at one point less on the mortgage than the church could otherwise get by borrowing the money through commercial institutions. And, where does PILP get its money? From individuals, from congregations, presbyteries, and synods; several General Assembly agencies have invested heavily. Those who invest will receive fair returns on their money, of course. Nothing against American Express, AT&T, or Coca-Cola, but as loyal Presbyterians, many would prefer having their money helping congregations in a cause that unites Presbyterians. (For more information, call 1-800-903-7457.) It is expected that it will be possible for people in all fifty states to participate by the time of the 1997 General Assembly.

New Church Development

We have noted that up until the end of World War II, new church developments were often initiated and implemented by "Old First Church" or some other congregation, and that was particularly the case when a church closer to town helped organize a new church in the same area, but farther away from downtown, perhaps in a new growing subdivision. Few particular churches have the means of either personnel or finances to do that kind of thing any longer, so a presbytery—usually aided by an arm of the General Assembly, such as the Evangelism and Church Development area of the National Ministries Division, or through PILP, described above—makes new church development possible. It just needs to be noted in passing that new church development is one of the extremely important things that we do together, and do well. Not many are concerned about the particular "theology" or bent that the new church will have—it will just be a Christian witness in a place where people are now residing.

Studies have shown that membership loss has been greater during the years in which there were fewer new church developments. One of the challenges at this time, of course, will be the concentration of new churches for ethnic minorities. The same principles are at work on church redevelopment projects, often, this time, at Old First Church itself. All of us work together in trying to provide and maintain a worthwhile and valuable ministry in a place that for any one of a number of reasons may not be able to be financially self-sustaining. But, once more, let us celebrate our significant cooperation.

Women are integrated into the life of the Presbyterian Church (U.S.A.)

One is tempted to say "fully integrated," but that would not quite be an accurate statement. It is a cause for celebration, however, and worth sending up rockets, that our denomination has come a very long way. We still give special note to the news that the first woman has become the president of a

Presbyterian seminary, and that the first woman has become the pastor of a church with more than 1,000 members, but there is more than a slight pause the first time someone hears that "[i]f the present seminary enrollment trends continue, women may well become a majority among Presbyterian ministers during the next century. . . . Inclusive language for people and for God may attract the most attention, but even more important has been the questioning of Christianity itself as hierarchical and patriarchal."[3]

Surely, no one any longer denigrates the tremendous contributions being made by women ministers, elders, and everyday church members. Many of us deeply regret that the church lost the often prophetic message and skilled leadership abilities that women could have provided in years gone by when they were denied these opportunities. Prejudice still exists against women as pastors of larger congregations, particularly, seemingly, among other women, so it behooves all of us to join together in working hard at the effort to be fully inclusive in having women in all kinds of leadership positions in the church and in society, as we strive, as well, for the same goals for ethnic minority persons.

Education

Education? That is surely old hat. Yes, but the hat has never gone out of style. The apostle Paul was no slouch as a teacher, so it is not unusual to find an appropriate reference:

> The gifts he gave were that some would be apostles, some prophets, some evangelists, some pastors and teachers, to equip the saints for the work of ministry, for building up the body of Christ, until all of us come to the unity of the faith and of the knowledge of the Son of God, to maturity, to the measure of the full stature of Christ.
> (Eph. 4:11–13)

Forgetting the matter of unity for the moment, there are several notes on this NRSV translation. (1) There is no comma between

"pastors" and "teachers." Interesting. (2) There *is* a comma between "teachers" and "to equip." Try reading the passage
without that comma and be thrilled. (3) Revel in the use of the
word "maturity," not something unattainable like "perfection." We skipped over the purpose of teaching in the church:
"for building up the body of Christ," which Paul in other
places calls the church. The ultimate objective is unambigu-
ous: "the knowledge of the Son of God."
What does John Calvin do with this passage?

We see that though God could easily make his [*sic*] people perfect in a single moment, yet it was not his will
that they should grow to mature age, but under the education of the Church. We see the means expressed; the
preaching of the heavenly doctrine is assigned to the
pastors. We see that all are placed under the same reg-
ulation, in order that they may submit themselves with
gentleness and docility of mind to be governed by the
pastors who are appointed for this purpose. . . . He not
only requires us to be attentive to reading, but has appointed teachers for our assistance. . . . Those who consider the authority of the doctrine as weakened by the
meanness of the men who are called to teach it, betray
their ingratitude; because among so many excellent
gifts with which God has adorned mankind, it is a peculiar privilege, that he deigns to consecrate men's lips
and tongues to his service, that his voice may be heard
in them.[4]

While a strong emphasis on education is not peculiar to
Presbyterians, it is distinctive because more colleges were
founded early by Presbyterians in this country than by any
other single denomination. Presbyterian General Assem-
blies have also repeatedly strongly endorsed public education, but that predilection also comes from Calvin. In
Geneva the Academy that Calvin established was for all,
and though it is not certain that women were included, from
Calvin's correspondence with women it can be extrapolated

that he truly advocated universal education. Interestingly, one of the early developments in materials for Sunday schools was another one of those parachurch efforts in the production of what were called the "Uniform Lessons" for all age groups from toddlers through adults. In addition to schools and colleges, twelve theological seminaries and the Presbyterian School of Christian Education are related to our denomination within the United States, plus the Evangelical Seminary of Puerto Rico, and many more around the world.

The point of all of this is crystal clear. Based on biblical principles and Reformed theology, the Presbyterian Church has always insisted on an educated professional ministry, for the sound reason that pastors are the first teachers of scripture and theology for all church members, and the people should be taught well by trained and skilled persons who are committed and dedicated to Jesus Christ as Savior. If one basic principle has united Presbyterians from their first days on these shores, it has been the fundamental value and necessity of quality education, and the first purpose was always based on the concept of the priesthood of all believers: each Christian should be able to read and comprehend the scriptures for her or his own maturing faith.

Our ties are strong
across the globe

Annually some 75 persons from partner churches overseas serve as "missionaries to the U.S.A." in churches, seminaries, conference centers, and especially in one synod—the Synod of the Covenant—that cannot receive enough such persons. Eighty-five presbytery and two synod ongoing meaningful relationships have been established with presbyteries, or their equivalents, in partner churches in a variety of nations. On an experimental basis several presbyteries are seeking to work with the General Assembly Council's Worldwide Ministries Division in recruiting and funding missionaries.

The Presbyterian Church
(U.S.A.) Foundation

An astute session of a not-to-be-named church is making the minimum payments on a building loan, but more is being received in that church than the amount of the mortgage payments. Any available balance is being sent to the Presbyterian Foundation for investment, and that church is earning more from the Foundation than it is required to pay on the loan. All across the church, individuals and governing bodies give money to the Presbyterian Foundation, and the income from the investment is used for mission purposes at the discretion of the fund donor.

All of the General Assembly endowments received through the years for both general and specific mission causes are held by the Foundation, and the income is being used for the designated mission purpose stated by the donor. Some of those endowments were made one hundred and more years ago. An ever-increasing number of churches and presbyteries are availing themselves of the services of the Presbyterian Foundation for safeguarding investments.

The Presbyterian Foundation is one of the oldest and largest church foundations anywhere. Over one billion dollars are invested with the Foundation for mission.

The Presbyterian
Publishing Corporation

Westminster Press, John Knox Press (now together known as Westminster John Knox Press), and Geneva Press have published quality books for years for our denomination and for the entire Christian world, plus wholesome books for the general public, such as *The Gospel According to Peanuts*. A new venture for the Presbyterian Publishing Corporation, in addition to continuing to publish books under these imprints, is in making available to the Presbyterian Church (U.S.A.) a broad variety of ecumenical curriculum materials. It would be difficult, indeed, to find a reading Presbyterian who does not feel a special twinge of pride and delight in knowing that "our press" remains in the vanguard of making available books and resources for the Christian world. Sunday bulletins, *These Days* devotional magazine, *The Presbyterian Hymnal*, the popular *StoryTeller* vacation Bible school series, and an array of software products are among the Presbyterian Publishing Corporation's offerings.

One Key Effort in Social Outreach: The Ministry of Medicine

In earlier times it was more obvious than it is now that the Presbyterian Church, as a nationwide entity, believes in ministering to the whole person, and a primary illustration of that conviction was through medical mission, in addition to education. Presbyterian-related hospitals still exist in New York, Chicago, and San Francisco, and through such groups as Presbyterian Medical Services in the Southwest. Medical mission around the world has been a hallmark of Presbyterian outreach; there are still over 125 Presbyterian Church (U.S.A.)–related hospitals, clinics, and nursing schools on our planet.

If we are inclined to conclude that Presbyterians have abandoned medical mission, we may need to reflect upon what is actually happening today. Several illustrations follow.

1. Retirement Homes and Health Centers. There are numerous retirement homes sponsored wholly or in part by some arm of the Presbyterian Church. If elderly people have more need for medical care than any other population group, a person can readily comprehend the medical requirements for residents of these communities. With the general population living longer it is imperative to keep senior citizens as well as possible, in part, quite frankly, to reduce the financial burden on families and on younger people everywhere.

2. Community Centers. The long-established as well as the more recently developed community centers related to our church, increasingly, again, have clinics or other medical programs for lower-income citizens. Well-baby clinics have long been a staple of some community centers, but such things as blood pressure testing and guidance on healthy eating, proper dieting, general nutrition, and the like, are relatively easily provided and inexpensive to offer.

3. Wellness Programs. Instead of emphasizing nursing homes or health centers in the Presbyterian-related clinics and retirement facilities, more and more attention is being given to "assisted living" programs so that residents can continue living in their own residences or in basic assisted living programs, without having to enter a nursing home, where they are removed from family, friends, the "old neighborhood," and the church community.

A striking feature in a few larger churches is having a Wellness Committee, or even a "Wellness" staff person, or a parish nurse. Their position descriptions differ from place to place, but the desirability of emphasizing health in a Christian context once more binds us together in a new way on an old subject. What we are seeing is a not-so-gradual transition, a move away from a lifetime commitment to medical treatment and a move toward illness prevention in such seemingly disparate situations as mission hospitals overseas and local congregations in the United States.

Although the hoped-for achievements are quite different from those of a hundred, fifty, or even twenty-five years ago, the concern is virtually identical: mission to the whole person through medical practice. The outstanding virtue of the newer approach, aside from the goal of having people stay well longer and participate more productively in their daily routines, is that few congregations or even presbyteries today could possibly charter a hospital, but even very small congregations could have wellness seminars, discussion groups, and studies for various age groups. While sponsoring the wellness principle in nurturing their own community of faith, they would also achieve a mission goal in the health field in the area where the church is located. For over forty years the Presbyterian

Health, Education, and Welfare Association has sought to emphasize, coordinate, resource, and support the various denominational efforts in these vital and important areas, plus related endeavors, in the life of the church.

> There is a balm in Gilead to make the wounded whole.
> There is a balm in Gilead to heal the sin-sick soul.

Sometimes I feel discouraged,
And think my work's in vain,
But then the Holy Spirit
Revives my soul again.

> There is a balm in Gilead to make the wounded whole.
> There is a balm in Gilead to heal the sin-sick soul.

Don't ever feel discouraged,
For Jesus is your friend,
And if you lack for knowledge
He'll not refuse to lend.

> There is a balm in Gilead to make the wounded whole.
> There is a balm in Gilead to heal the sin-sick soul.

If you cannot preach like Peter,
If you cannot pray like Paul,
You can tell the love of Jesus
And say, "He died for all."

> There is a balm in Gilead to make the wounded whole.
> There is a balm in Gilead to heal the sin-sick soul.
>
> (African American Spiritual)[5]

13

"I Will Lift Up My Eyes"
Our Vision

"Paradise" comes from the Persian word *ferdows*, which means park or garden. The garden is surrounded by the desert, but inside the garden there is always a cool flowing stream, as well as singing birds, magnificent flowers, and glorious shade-producing trees. The Persian poets insist that there must also be a musical instrument, a jug of wine, and a beautiful maiden—one kind of vision. In contrast, the biblical garden has the tree of life in the midst of the glories of creation with the creator God, strolling in the garden in the cool of the day.

The final biblical vision is of even greater contrast. It is of an angel showing the river of the water of life, flowing from the throne of God and of the Lamb through the middle of the street of the city. On either side of the river is the tree of life, with its twelve kinds of fruit, whose leaves are for the healing of the nations. But that is only part of the vision. For there is a new heaven and a new earth with the holy city, the new Jerusalem, coming down from heaven, for the home of God is among mortals, and God will be with God's people![1]

The Gospel accounts are of a kingdom of God that is here and now, yet also to come fully in God's own time. Thus our visions are eternal in scope, but only partially revealed and understood now. The biblical writers depict the young as seeing visions and the old as dreaming dreams. There is a constant yearning for the future to be present. For our generation of Presbyterians we suggest three visions, or one vision in three parts.

For the Christian there is a calling from God, so that the vision for each person defines life; there is something that life is all about and for. There is purpose—and meaning.

    a. Our vision is of a church focusing on the essentials. Let us as a denomination rally around the "Great Ends of the Church." As noted earlier, the six General Assembly agencies are proposing this emphasis for six consecutive meetings of the General Assembly, 1998–2003. Our vision is that all of us in the church would give special attention to these subjects. The interaction could benefit us all in profound ways if we could have a united mission message to the world and to ourselves. We believe that this is possible.

    b. Our vision is of a church at peace with itself. Let us "box" the question posed by Rodney King, "Can't we all just get along?" In the churchwide debates and discussions on homosexuality, the good news is that we have talked biblically, theologically, and earnestly with each other, in some places for the first time in many years in such depth. The bad news is that we have faced serious division, and we have not always been civil with each other. Specific steps can be taken to improve markedly our church climate.

    c. Our vision is of a church alive in mission. We have received the gospel, not to keep to ourselves, but to share with all the world. Our dream is that the Presbyterian Church (U.S.A.) and all of its congregations and governing bodies will come alive with a new passion for mission—in our communities, in our nation, and throughout the world. That will not resolve all of our differences, but it will unite us together behind a larger purpose: God's purpose of salvation and reconciliation for the world.

    We believe that there are some hazards in proposing these three, or any three, visions, since any consideration of them could detract from other previously approved efforts that are either already underway locally or nationally or that are on the drawing board or about to be begun. But we are also convinced that our denomination is sufficiently at risk that some such common-ground possibilities are needed to bring us closer together sooner rather than later. It would be our hope and expectation that wherever any seeming conflicts arise between current and future programs, and any agreed-upon unifying tactics, that we might strive to do both, rather than eliminating either. One beauty of these three visions is that their implementation would not involve a large expenditure of money.

These three vision possibilities need to be fleshed out a bit.

Our vision is of a church focusing on the essentials

The Great Ends of the Church are: "the proclamation of the gospel for the salvation of humankind; the shelter, nurture, and spiritual fellowship of the children of God; the maintenance of divine worship; the preservation of the truth; the promotion of social righteousness; and the exhibition of the Kingdom of Heaven to the world" (G-1.0200).

Chapters IX, X, XI, XII, and XIII of the *Book of Order* begin in a way that is fascinating, in that there is a common theme running through these chapters on Governing Bodies, the Session, the Presbytery, the Synod, and the General Assembly, though the language is different in each chapter. The central theme at the beginning of each chapter is that each governing body is a unit of mission!

Of course there is no statement in the *Book of Order* that says the mission in each governing body should be the same. Although the mission is not identical from one governing body to another, the connectedness of the whole is apparent. There was a time when presbyteries and synods were required to establish their budgets "in the light of" their related governing bodies, indicating the very close ties.

Our vision is that with no compulsion from any source we might interact with each other on how we address the Great Ends of the Church. We could address them in both stating what they mean for *this* presbytery, *this* session, and so on, while painting a picture as to how the "Great Ends" might become increasingly meaningful at other mission responsibility levels, also.

Then let us share, and in that way our mosaic would be the coming together of all the parts like pieces fitting in a jigsaw puzzle. In a magnificent way we would see the total picture of what we are about as a united church. We could make suggestions and comments to each other about how better any one of us could fulfill and make real, and even enlarge, the blueprint that we have visualized (to change the metaphor), and according to which we have begun to build.

We are now looking to new ways across governing body structures to consider the use of mission income. Now, also, a General Assembly agency, a synod, or a presbytery may make funds available to a session to aid in major repairs as a result of a disaster or for new church development. Our vision is that we cooperate deliberately in reviewing the implications for *us*—wherever we are—and for *us as a whole church* as we study anew the Great Ends of the Church—and live them out!

Our focus on "the Great Ends" should also lead us afresh to the Book (the scriptures) and the books (our Constitution) on which they are based. To make "the Great Ends" come alive we need a new commitment to join together in serious study of the Bible, our *Book of Confessions*, and our *Book of Order*. Many benefited from the churchwide study of 1 Corinthians in 1996, and we hope that Presbyterians across the church will share in the forthcoming adult study on "the Great Ends" being developed by the Congregational Ministries Division. At a time when so many Presbyterians have little or no Presbyterian background personally, the Bible, as vital as it is, should not remain the only subject for deep study. Pastors could preach and teach Reformed theology and polity as well, including an emphasis on such things as the historic and important role of education for all Christians, particularly our own members. A series of seminars on the Presbyterian Church, its theology, worship, polity, and mission, to name a few possible subjects for exploration, could be offered at select locations across the church.

Our vision is of a church
at peace with itself

The kicking and beating of Rodney King by some Los Angeles police officers a few years ago was recorded on film by a witness. When that video and other evidence were not deemed sufficient by the jury to convict the alleged offenders, a riot, largely along racial lines, erupted. There was great destruction of property, and rifts developed everywhere among ethnic communities. Seeing with horror the mayhem that resulted from the incident, the initial victim asked in plaintive tones, "Can't we all just get along?" Racism is alive and well in our land, and we need to combat racism. The question and the feeling behind it are being posed here for factions within the Presbyterian Church (U.S.A.). Instead of police clubs and weapons of physical harm we are much more likely to use words, written and verbal, to tear asunder the soul of both victim and perpetrator.

Being at peace does not mean agreeing on everything. Churches can be at peace while vigorously debating and discussing the issues that count, strongly disagreeing on occasion. Surely, we dare not leave unaddressed the recent "rending of the body of clay" we have wrought over the subject of homosexuality. It is perfectly appropriate for us to disagree on matters of such consequence, but one wonders how we can justify our wounding those most directly affected on both sides of such issues, and how we can tolerate any conduct unbecoming the body of Christ in the process of our discussions. The time for candor all around has arrived.

Let us be honest with one another and, in some instances, say, "You and I agree on this matter, but I don't think you were civil or courteous with the other side. It seems to me that you and I and those who share our thinking have some bridges to build with those who were our 'opponents.'" The apostle Paul had some relevant thoughts:

If we live by the Spirit, let us also be guided by the Spirit.

Let us not become conceited, competing against one another, envying one another.

My friends, if anyone is detected in a transgression, you who have received the Spirit should restore such a one in a spirit of gentleness. Take care that you yourselves are not tempted. Bear one another's burdens, and in this way you will fulfill the law of Christ. For if those who are nothing think they are something, they deceive themselves. . . . So then, whenever we have an opportunity, let us work for the good of all, and especially for those of the family of faith. (Gal. 5:25–6:3, 10)

In a time of healing, very few genuine attempts to put balm on wounds can succeed without confession and forgiveness. Many of us are not experts in taking actions of confession, healing, or forgiveness, so we may need to extend ourselves beyond our normal patterns of behavior, demanding *genuine* efforts of ourselves. Gays and lesbians, as well as those who are convinced that scriptural authority is being breached, must be in continuing conversation and joint relationships of one kind or another. Warm hearts and pastoral spirits are needed as never before in the Presbyterian Church (U.S.A.).

We make no apology for urging our spending time, thought, and effort to the matter of internal healing, spiritual reflection, and biblical and theological study about ourselves and how we can more truly be the church. We are not navelgazing. Benton Johnson has stated that the Presbyterian Church (U.S.A.) "needs to develop . . . [an] agenda aimed at revitalizing itself as a religious institution and to assign this task a very high priority in the critical period just ahead."[2]

The attention of the church is called to the document *Seeking to Be Faithful Together: Guidelines for Presbyterians During Times of Disagreement*, adopted by the 204th General Assembly (1992).[3] A number of strategic steps for keeping in touch with each other as we confront our differences are listed in this document.

Our vision is of a church
alive in mission

During the civil rights struggle in the South, the city of Atlanta adopted the slogan, "A City Too Busy to Hate." The purpose was to encourage all Atlantans, black and white, to be busy building up the city as the capital of the New South, rather than focusing on old wounds and prejudices. In the process it was hoped that as people from all races and conditions of life pulled together behind a common purpose they would develop mutual respect and appreciation for one another.

Our dream for the Presbyterian Church (U.S.A.) is that we will be a church so busy in mission that we literally won't have the time or energy for much of the divisiveness and conflict that characterize our church today. We hope that every congregation and every governing body will make a fresh commitment to sharing the gospel in word and deed in their own community and throughout the world. As we join together as a missionary people, determined to make a difference for the gospel in the world, we are confident that we will gain a new respect and love for one another.

It has been done before! It is hard to imagine any group more diverse than the group assembled in Jerusalem on that first Pentecost. They came from literally every continent, every race, and every social condition known in the Mediterranean world. Yet when they received the Holy Spirit, they set out with a passion for mission. As the book of Acts makes clear, their differences did not disappear, but they found a new bond in a higher calling. They literally "turned the world upside down" for the sake of the gospel. With a fresh commitment among Presbyterians that the world which God loves comes first in our life, we believe the Presbyterian Church (U.S.A.) can find renewal, community, and—even more important—"turn the world upside down" for the sake of the gospel.

We hope that every local congregation and every governing body will make a fresh commitment to being a missionary

society. Our communities and the world need as never before
to hear and believe the good news of the gospel:

> that in Christ all can have life, and that abundantly;
> that God intends food for the hungry, a cup of cold
> water for the thirsty, and compassion for those in
> need;
> that in Christ there is neither Jew nor Greek, slave
> nor free, male nor female, but that all the world
> can be one; and
> that even swords can be beaten into plowshares and
> the world can know peace.

This is the hope of the world and the fundamental calling of
the Presbyterian Church (U.S.A.). It is also the ultimate truth
we know in the life, death and resurrection of Jesus Christ. If
we as a church can find common ground in this mission, there
is indeed bright hope for the future of the Presbyterian Church
(U.S.A.) and for the world God loves.

A Brief Statement of Faith—
Presbyterian Church (U.S.A.)

In life and in death we belong to God.
    Through the grace of our Lord Jesus Christ,
        the love of God,
            and the communion of the Holy Spirit,
    we trust in the one triune God, the Holy One of Israel,
        whom alone we worship and serve.

We trust in Jesus Christ,
    fully human, fully God.
    Jesus proclaimed the reign of God:
        preaching good news to the poor
        and release to the captives,
        teaching by word and deed
        and blessing the children,

healing the sick
  and binding up the brokenhearted,
 eating with outcasts,
 forgiving sinners,
 and calling on all to repent and believe the gospel.
Unjustly condemned for blasphemy and sedition,
Jesus was crucified,
  suffering the depths of human pain
  and giving his life for the sins of the world.
God raised this Jesus from the dead,
 vindicating his sinless life,
 breaking the power of sin and evil,
 delivering us from death to life eternal.

We trust in God,
 whom Jesus called Abba, Father.
In sovereign love God created the world good
 and makes everyone equally in God's image,
  male and female, of every race and people,
 to live as one community.
But we rebel against God; we hide from our Creator.
 Ignoring God's commandments,
  we violate the image of God in others and ourselves,
 accept lies as truth,
 exploit neighbor and nature,
 and threaten death to the plant entrusted to our care.
 We deserve God's condemnation.
Yet God acts with justice and mercy to redeem creation.
 In everlasting love,
  the God of Abraham and Sarah chose a covenant people
   to bless all families of the earth.
 Hearing their cry,
  God delivered the children of Israel
   from the house of bondage.
 Loving us still,
  God makes us heirs with Christ of the covenant.
 Like a mother who will not forsake her nursing child,

like a father who runs to welcome the prodigal home,
God is faithful still.

We trust in God the Holy Spirit,
everywhere the giver and renewer of life.
The Spirit justifies us by grace through faith,
sets us free to accept ourselves and to love God and
neighbor,
and binds us together with all believers
in the one body of Christ, the Church.
The same Spirit
who inspired the prophets and apostles
rules our faith and life in Christ through Scripture,
engages us through the Word proclaimed,
claims us in the waters of baptism,
feeds us with the bread of life and the cup of salvation,
and calls women and men to all ministries of the Church.
In a broken and fearful world
the Spirit gives us courage
to pray without ceasing,
to witness among all peoples to Christ as Lord and Savior,
to unmask idolatries in Church and culture,
to hear the voices of peoples long silenced,
and to work with others for justice, freedom, and peace.
In gratitude to God, empowered by the Spirit,
we strive to serve Christ in our daily tasks
and to live holy and joyful lives,
even as we watch for God's new heaven and new earth,
praying, "Come, Lord Jesus!"

With believers in every time and place,
we rejoice that nothing in life or in death
can separate us from the love of God in Christ Jesus our Lord.

Glory be to the Father, and to the Son, and to the Holy Spirit.
Amen.[4]

Notes

Chapter 1:
The Need for Common Ground

1. Eugene H. Peterson, *The Message* (Colorado Springs, Colo.: Nav-Press, 1993), 227.

2. Roland H. Bainton, *Here I Stand: A New Life of Martin Luther* (New York: New Amsterdam Library, 1995), 144.

3. *The Constitution of the Presbyterian Church (U.S.A.)*, Part I: *Book of Confessions* (Louisville, Ky.: Office of the General Assembly, 1991), sections 6, 7, and 8.

4. James H. Smylie, *A Brief History of the Presbyterians* (Louisville, Ky.: Geneva Press, 1996), 45.

5. Lefferts A. Loetscher, *A Brief History of the Presbyterians*, 4th ed. (Philadelphia: Westminster Press, 1983), 64.

6. Ibid., 77.

7. Ibid., 135.

8. "Called to Be Catholic," prepared by the National Pastoral Life Center, 18 Bleecker St., New York, NY 10012.

9. Ibid.

10. Ibid.

11. Peterson, *The Message* (Romans 15:1–2).

12. John H. Leith, *An Introduction to the Reformed Tradition: A Way of Being the Christian Community*, rev. ed. (Atlanta: John Knox Press, 1981), 53–54.

13. Samuel John Stone, "The Church's One Foundation," in *The Presbyterian Hymnal* (Louisville, Ky.: Westminster/John Knox Press, 1990), no. 442.

Chapter 2:
Our Reformed Heritage

1. Leith, *Introduction to the Reformed Tradition*, 7.
2. See Habakkuk 2:4; Romans 1:7; Galatians 3:11.
3. Douglas F. Ottati, *Reforming Protestantism: Christian Commitment in Today's World* (Louisville, Ky.: Westminster John Knox Press, 1995), 3.
4. *Book of Confessions*, Section 6.
5. Leith, *Introduction to the Reformed Tradition*, 72.
6. Ibid.
7. *Book of Confessions*, Section 7, Question 1.
8. Ottati, *Reforming Protestantism*, 3.
9. Leith, *Introduction to the Reformed Tradition*, 74.
10. John Calvin, *Institutes of the Christian Religion*, 1.7.4 (Philadelphia: Presbyterian Board of Christian Education, 1936), volume I, page 90.
11. John Calvin, "I Greet Thee, Who My Sure Redeemer Art," in *The Presbyterian Hymnal*, no. 457.

Chapter 3:
Our Constitutional Heritage

1. *The Constitution of the Presbyterian Church (U.S.A.)*, Part II: *Book of Order* (Louisville, Ky.: Office of the General Assembly of the Presbyterian Church (U.S.A.), 1996).
2. Cynthia M. Campbell, in Joan S. Gray and Joyce C. Tucker, *Presbyterian Polity for Church Officers*, 2d ed. (Louisville, Ky.: John Knox Press, 1990), xii.
3. Some may prefer "the reign" of Jesus Christ to "the Lordship."
4. Hugh T. Kerr, ed., *A Compend of the Institutes of the Christian Religion by John Calvin* (Philadelphia: Westminster Press, 1939), 153.
5. Smylie, *A Brief History*, 23.
6. *Book of Confessions*, 4.001.
7. Dean R. Hoge and David A. Roozen, eds., *Understanding Church Growth and Decline, 1950–1978* (New York: Pilgrim Press, 1979), 21–159, 179–223, 315–33; W. Clark and William McKinney, *American Mainline Religion: Its Changing Shape and Future* (New Brunswick, N.J.: Rutgers University Press, 1987), 106–85.
8. James L. Mays, *Psalms*, Interpretation (Louisville, Ky.: John Knox Press, 1994), 318–19.

9. Ibid.

10. *Book of Order*, "Directory for Worship," Preface, a.

11. Milton J Coalter, John M. Mulder, and Louis B. Weeks, eds., *The Re-Forming Tradition: Presbyterians and Mainstream Protestantism* (Louisville, Ky.: Westminster/John Knox Press, 1992), 97.

12. Loetscher, *A Brief History*, 94.

13. Ibid., 151.

14. Ibid., 118.

15. Ibid., 133.

16. Smylie, *A Brief History*, 123.

17. Donald K. McKim, *Westminster Dictionary of Theological Terms* (Louisville, Ky.: Westminster John Knox Press, 1996), 154.

18. A footnote in this section in the *Book of Order* states: "The words 'men' and 'man's' throughout this quotation from the eighteenth century should be understood as applying to all persons."

19. William Walsham How, "For All the Saints," in *The Presbyterian Hymnal*, no. 526.

Chapter 4:
The Church and Its Confessions

1. See the *Book of Order*, G-2.0000.

2. *Book of Confessions*. See the *Book of Order*, G-1.0500.

3. Jack Rogers, *Presbyterian Creeds: A Guide to the Book of Confessions* (Louisville, Ky.: Westminster/John Knox Press, 1991), 23-24.

4. See Edward A. Dowey, Jr., *A Commentary on the Confession of 1967 and An Introduction to the Book of Confessions* (Philadelphia: Westminster Press, 1968). Dowey chaired the Special Committee that produced the Confession of 1967 (sometimes called C-67).

5. Jack Rogers, *Presbyterian Creeds*, 231–32. Rogers was a member of the Special Committee that produced A Brief Statement of Faith. The "Brief Statement" received final approval in 1991.

6. George S. Hendry, "Christology," in *A Dictionary of Christian Theology*, ed. Alan Richardson (Philadelphia: Westminster Press, 1969), 55–56.

7. *Biblical Authority and Interpretation*, Report Received by the 194th General Assembly (1982), 34 (see chap. 7, note 3).

8. Dowey, *Commentary*, 175.

9. Rogers, *Presbyterian Creeds*, 104–5.

10. Ibid., 126.

11. F. L. Cross, ed., *The Oxford Dictionary of the Christian Church* (London: Oxford University Press, 1958), 132.

12. Rogers, *Presbyterian Creeds*, 212.

13. Isaac Watts, "Our God, Our Help in Ages Past," in *The Presbyterian Hymnal*, no. 210.

Chapter 5:
The Church and Its Mission

1. *Book of Order*, G-3.0000.

2. E. H. Gillett, *History of the Presbyterian Church in the United States of America*, Part II (rev. ed., Philadelphia: Presbyterian Board of Publication and Sabbath School Work, 1864), 513.

3. Peterson, *The Message*, 73.

4. John Fawcett, "Blest Be the Tie That Binds," in *The Presbyterian Hymnal*, no. 438.

Chapter 6:
The Church and Its Unity

1. The *Book of Order*, G-4.0000.

2. Robert McAfee Brown, "I Am Presbyterian—Therefore I Am Ecumenical," *Presbyterian Survey*, September 1987, 13–15.

3. Stone, "The Church's One Foundation," in *The Presbyterian Hymnal*, no. 442.

4. See W. Stanley Rycroft, *The Ecumenical Witness of the United Presbyterian Church in the U.S.A.* ([Philadelphia]: Board of Christian Education of the United Presbyterian Church in the U.S.A., 1968); Donald Black, *Merging Mission and Unity* (Philadelphia: Geneva Press, 1986); and "Report of the Ecumenical Consultation, 1975." Atlanta: Office of the Stated Clerk, Presbyterian Church in the U.S., 1975).

5. Coalter, Mulder, and Weeks, eds., *The Re-Forming Tradition*, 185.

6. World Council of Churches Central Committee, *Toward a Common Understanding and Vision of the World Council of Churches: A Working Draft of a Policy Statement* (Geneva: World Council of Churches, 1996), 29.

7. Ibid.

8. S. Mark Heim, "The Next Ecumenical Movement," *Christian Century*, August 14–21, 1996, 783.

9. *Minutes of the 208th General Assembly (1996) of the Presbyterian Church (U.S.A)*, Part I: *Journal* (Louisville, Ky.: Office of the General

Assembly, 1996), 53.

10. Ibid., 378.

11. Jane Parker Huber, "Called as Partners in Christ's Service," in *The Presbyterian Hymnal*, no. 343.

Chapter 7:
The Centrality of the Scriptures

1. *Book of Order*, G-14.0207b and G-14.0405b(2).

2. *Book of Confessions*, 9.27.

3. This report, *Biblical Authority and Interpretation*, is a resource document received by the 194th General Assembly (1982) of the United Presbyterian Church U.S.A. It cannot be purchased separately, but is the second half of a booklet titled *Presbyterian Understanding and Use of Holy Scripture*. The first half of the booklet (and giving the booklet its title) is a position statement adopted by the 123rd General Assembly (1983) of the Presbyterian Church in the U.S. The booklet (#OGA-92-03) is available from Presbyterian Distribution Service, 100 Witherspoon St., Louisville, KY 40202-1396 (telephone 800-524-2612 or, in Louisville, 502-569-5000, ext. 2503).

4. Ibid., 52.

5. See Randolph Crump Miller, *Biblical Theology and Christian Education* (New York: Charles Scribner's Sons, 1956).

6. *Biblical Authority and Interpretation*, 52.

7. Ibid.

8. Ibid.

9. Ibid.

10. Kenneth J. Foreman, "What Is the Bible?" in *The Layman's Bible Commentary*, vol. 1: *Introduction to the Bible* (Richmond: John Knox Press, 1959), 7–31.

11. Ibid., 7–31.

12. Ibid., 8.

13. Mary A. Lathbury, "Break Thou the Bread of Life," in *The Presbyterian Hymnal*, no. 329.

Chapter 8:
Reformed Worship

1. Leith, *Introduction to the Reformed Tradition*, 175.

2. Smylie, *A Brief History*, 20.

3. Ibid., 20–21.

4. Ibid., 21.
5. *Book of Common Worship* (Louisville, Ky.: Westminster/John Knox Press, 1993), 1034.
6. *Book of Order*, W-2.4006.
7. Ibid., W-3.3507.
8. Ibid., W-3.1002.
9. Hugh Thomson Kerr, "God of Our Life," in *The Presbyterian Hymnal*, no. 275.

Chapter 9:
Our Mission Challenge

1. Basil Mathews, *Forward through the Ages* (New York, N.Y.: Friendship Press, 1951), 115.
2. Smylie, *A Brief History*, 89.
3. G. Thompson Brown, *Presbyterians in World Mission: A Handbook for Congregations* (Decatur, Ga.: CTS Press, 1988), 7–8.
4. H. McKennie Goodpasture, ed., *Cross and Sword: An Eyewitness History of Christianity in Latin America* (Maryknoll, N.Y.: Orbis Books, 1989).
5. See Howard Zinn, *A People's History of the United States* (New York, N.Y.: Harper & Row, Harper Perennial, 1980).
6. Coalter, Mulder, and Weeks, eds., *The Re-Forming Tradition*, 156.
7. Smylie, *A Brief History*, 50.
8. William Warren Sweet, *The Story of Religion in America* (New York: Harper & Brothers, 1950), 361.
9. Louis B. Weeks, *Kentucky Presbyterians* (Atlanta: John Knox Press, 1983), 128–34.
10. Dean K. Thompson, "The Whitmans: Missionary Martyrs," in James H. Smylie, Dean K. Thompson, and Cary Patrick, *Go Therefore* (Atlanta: Presbyterian Publishing House, 1987), 1–9.
11. Everett N. Hunt, Jr., "John Livingstone Nevius," in *Mission Legacies*, ed. Gerald H. Anderson et al. (Maryknoll, N.Y.: Orbis Press, 1994), 190ff.
12. See James H. Smylie, "Robert E. Speer," in Smylie et al., *Go Therefore*, 46ff.; and Bradley J. Longfield, *The Presbyterian Controversy* (New York: Oxford University Press, 1991).
13. James H. Smylie, "Sheppard and Morrison: African Mission and Justice," in Smylie et al., *Go Therefore*, 37–45.
14. Dean K. Thompson, "Pearl Buck: Novels of Missionary Life," in Smylie et al., *Go Therefore*, 92–100.

15. Jeffery W. Rowthorn, "Lord, You Give the Great Commission," *The Presbyterian Hymnal*, no. 429.

Chapter 10:
The Particular Church

1. Milton J Coalter et al., eds., *Vital Signs: The Promise of Mainstream Protestantism* (Grand Rapids: Wm. B. Eerdmans Publishing Co., 1996, 81–82.

2. "The Healing Church," pamphlet from the Stewardship and Communication Development Unit of the Presbyterian Church (U.S.A.), 1991.

3. Coalter, Mulder, and Weeks, eds., *The Re-Forming Tradition*, 113.

4. Louis B. Weeks and William Fogleman, "A Two-Church Hypothesis," *Presbyterian Outlook*, no. 172 (March 26, 1990): 8.

5. *Book of Order*, G-9.0409.

6. Ibid., G-11.0103.

7. Ibid., G-10.0102.

8. *Vital Signs*, 104.

9. Benton Johnson, "On Dropping the Subject: Presbyterians and Sabbath Observance in the Twentieth Century" in Milton J Coalter, John M. Mulder, and Louis B. Weeks, eds., *The Presbyterian Predicament: Six Perspectives* (Louisville, Ky.: Westminster/John Knox Press, 1990), 107–8.

10. Ibid., 108.

11. Leonard Sweet, "Can Mainstream Change Its Course?" in Robert S. Michaelson and Wade Clark Roof, eds., *Liberal Protestantism* (New York: Pilgrim Press, 1986), 243.

12. Grayson L. Tucker, "Enhancing Church Vitality through Congregational Identity Change," in Milton J Coalter, John M. Mulder, and Louis B. Weeks, eds., *The Mainstream Protestant "Decline": The Presbyterian Pattern* (Louisville, Ky.: Westminster/John Knox Press, 1990), 73–74.

13. Ibid., 74.

14. Ibid., 68.

15. See chapters V, VI, and VII in the Form of Government, and W-1.1406 and W-2.1004 in the Directory for Worship, in the *Book of Order*.

16. Timothy Dwight, "I Love Thy Kingdom, Lord," in *The Presbyterian Hymnal*, no. 441.

Chapter 11:
Our Polity

1. *Book of Order*, G-11.0103x.
2. Ibid., G-11.0103b.
3. Ibid., G-11.0103e.
4. Ibid., G-11.0103f.
5. Ibid., G-11.0103g.
6. Ibid., G-1.0100b.
7. Calvin, *Institutes*, vol. II, 434.
8. *Book of Order*, G-1.0307.
9. David Little, *Religion, Order, and Law: A Study in Pre-Revolutionary England* (New York: Harper & Row, 1969), 68.
10. Martin Luther, "A Mighty Fortress Is Our God," in *The Presbyterian Hymnal*, no. 260.

Chapter 12:
Our Vast Array of Realities of Unity

1. *Mission Yearbook for Prayer and Study*, 1996, p. 373.
2. Alexa Smith, "Presbyterians Explore High-Technology Witnessing on the Outskirts of the Magic Kingdom," *PresbyNews*, Dec. 21, 1996. Also published in *News Briefs: Presbyterian Church (U.S.A.)*, no. 9652 (Dec. 27, 1996), 9–11.
3. Coalter, Mulder, and Weeks, eds., *The Re-Forming Tradition*, 111.
4. Calvin, *Institutes* 4.1.5.
5. "There Is a Balm in Gilead," in *The Presbyterian Hymnal*, no. 394.

Chapter 13:
Our Vision

1. See Genesis 1—2 and Revelation 21—22.
2. Benton Johnson, "From Old to New Agendas: Presbyterians and Social Issues in the Twentieth Century," in Milton J Coalter, John M. Mulder, and Louis B. Weeks, eds., *The Confessional Mosaic: Presbyterians and Twentieth-Century Theology* (Louisville, Ky.: Westminster/John Knox Press, 1990), 234–35.
3. *Seeking to Be Faithful Together: Guidelines for Presbyterians During Times of Disagreement* (4 pages), a document adopted by the 204th General Assembly (1992), is published in several adaptations and in

three languages. The adaptation for use by sessions and congregations (English language) (#DMS 259-93-928) is, like the others, available from Presbyterian Distribution Service (see chap. 7, note 3, for address).

4. "A Brief Statement of Faith—Presbyterian Church (U.S.A.)," Office of the General Assembly, 1990; included in the *Book of Confessions* (section 10), beginning with the 1991 edition.

Index